The Weapons of a Warrior is a must-read for believers of all ages and backgrounds. Pastor JoAnne Ramsay lays out step by step how every believer can be an overcomer when facing spiritual warfare. This handbook outlines important keys for every soldier of the faith to overcome opposition and come into their full potential in Christ.

Rev. Danette Crawford

Founder and President, Joy Ministries Evangelistic Association, Inc.
Television Host of *Hope for Today with Danette Crawford*

This is not a book of abstract concepts contrived to convey ideals that are merely hopeful and theoretical; nor is it a collection of mystical experiences intended to amaze the reader. *The Weapons of a Warrior* contains a practical and very real handbook for God's soldier. These essential truths were not espoused from the lofty towers of academia, nor stumbled upon in the laboratory of experimentation; they were tested and proven in the field of battle. I am personally acquainted with the author and can testify that she is not only a teacher of God's Word, but a practitioner of these powerful principles. The experiences shared and lessons learned through this handbook will equip and enable every believer who practices them to a greater dimension of victory! "Death and life are in the power of the tongue: and they that love it shall eat the fruit thereof" (Proverbs 18:21 KJV).

Rev. John Blanchard, MDiv

Senior Pastor, Rock Church International, Virginia Beach, VA

From the introduction to the final chapter, *The Weapons of a Warrior*, by my friend, Pastor JoAnne Ramsay, is without question one of the greatest encouragements to the Body of Christ to stand on faith and be bold in prayer! Pastor Jo speaks to the heart of believers and motivates them to decree and declare God's Word from the place of victory. *The Weapons of a Warrior* reminds the Body of Christ that

God's Word has the power within itself to do exactly what God has sent it to do. It encouraged me, as it will you, to take the limits off God and remember to always speak the Word because our victory is in our mouth!

Dorothy Spalding
President and Founder, Watchmen Broadcasting, Augusta, GA

The

WEAPONS
of a WARRIOR

A Soldier's Handbook
for Spiritual Warfare

PASTOR JOANNE RAMSAY

Fruitbearer Publishing LLC
Georgetown, DE

The Weapons of a Warrior: A Soldier's Handbook for Spiritual Warfare
Copyright © 2018 by JoAnne Ramsay. All rights reserved.
ISBN: 978-1-938796-46-3
Library of Congress Control Number: 2018931137
Cover Design: Sarah Welker (design-beast.com) with Candy Abbott

Published by Fruitbearer Publishing
P.O. Box 777
Georgetown, DE 19947
www.fruitbearer.com

Published in Georgetown, Delaware, by Fruitbearer Publishing LLC.

First Edition

Printed in the United States of America

Acknowledgments

First and foremost, I want to thank the Lord for His unfailing, unconditional love for me. Thank You, Lord, for saving my soul and allowing me the awesome privilege of ministering and teaching Your people. I want to give You all the glory, for without the inspiration of the Holy Spirit who gave me these messages, I would not have been able to write this book.

To my husband, David: thank you for your faith in me and for encouraging me to write this book. Thank you for being my rock. Thank you for your patience and understanding as I spent many hours putting together the content in this book. I thank God for you, for you truly are a gift from God.

To my family and friends: thank you for believing in me and encouraging me as I seek to fulfill God's calling on my life and as I walk in obedience to write every book the Lord has placed on my heart to write.

A special thank you to Danette Crawford of Joy Ministries, for her prayers and encouragement—a woman after God's own heart.

A huge thank you to Hope Flinchbaugh, who heard God's voice and shifted her workload so she could help me with this book, and for her tireless patience in getting me through to the finish.

A big thank you to Larry Nevenhoven, who spent countless hours listening to my messages and watching my videos so he could give life to this book.

To my precious partners: thank you for your generous gifts of time, prayer, and financial support. Thank you! Together, we are transforming lives one WORD at a time. Thank you for listening to Speak the Word ministry and for applying the principles of my teachings to your lives. May the Lord continue to give you revelation of His Word.

Contents

Foreword

Welcome to a wonderful handbook for the busy warrior of Christ! I know this book will speak directly to your heart.

We all fight battles every day and this world is not kind, but this book helps us to hear God's Word and take practical steps to ensure victory against the devil. Pastor JoAnne Ramsay lays out exactly what to say, by faith from God's Word, to win the war against evil.

I have known Pastor Jo for twenty-five years; she is everything she says she is. I have watched the Spirit of God grow in her and seen first-hand how He has changed her. Through all her experiences of life—marriage, business, child-rearing, personal relationships—she has held onto and grown in her faith. I am proud to call Jo a sister in faith and a friend in God.

Throughout my years in business, I have read many self-help books, each offering advice on what to say or how to speak. Read on and you will discover that this is the last self-help book you will ever need. Whether you are dealing with kids, a spouse, or business colleagues, the answers are here. Pastor Jo tells you about the power of your words in everyday life. This book will arm you for battle against the enemy who lurks around every corner, trying to invade our thoughts and actions thousands of times a day.

The Weapons of a Warrior: A Soldier's Handbook for Spiritual Warfare, is a frank and practical study of the Word of God. This book will help you fight through a minor problem or a life-changing crisis. Whether you are a Bible scholar or a new believer, you will grow in the Word of God and, therefore, in your relationship with God.

In the latest *Iron Man* movie, Tony Stark calls his armor to him, piece by piece, until he is invincible to the bad guys. In the same way, Pastor Jo teaches you how to put on the armor of Christ and to speak the armor of God to each part of your body. She tells us how to hold our Father in remembrance to His words to us, the armor of God's Word that saves us from all evil.

Indeed, our victory is in our mouths.

Thank you, Pastor Jo, for showing me how to arm myself with the promises of God's Word, to put on His armor, and to become a warrior of God. May we fight alongside each other for many years to come.

Anne Derby
Derby Consulting

Preface

A few years ago, I stood in our kitchen talking to my husband, David, about my ministry when the Holy Spirit burst into our midst, blanketing me with His presence. His nearness almost made me weep. The Holy Spirit whispered to my heart, each word fueled with urgency and anguish.

He said that believers have been in a spiritual war against the kingdom of darkness since the Garden of Eden. The battle has not lessened one bit over time and continues stronger than ever today. He said that most of His children do not know how to fight spiritual battles, and if they are not taught, they will continue losing battles— ones they should have won.

The Holy Spirit referred to believers as His soldiers.

Spiritual warfare? Soldiers of the Lord?

These expressions may sound a little over the top for those who think believers must always bend over backward to accept what is happening in their lives. The Apostle Paul, however, certainly did not agree with that attitude:

> Put on the whole armor of God, that you may be able to stand against the wiles of the devil. For we do not wrestle against flesh and blood, but against principalities, against powers, against the rulers of the darkness of this age, against spiritual hosts of wickedness in the heavenly places. (Ephesians 6:11–12)

THE WEAPONS OF A WARRIOR

Throughout his letters, Paul often referred to believers as soldiers and their struggles as warfare against the devil. He even defined the soldier's armor:

> Therefore take up the whole armor of God, that you may be able to withstand in the evil day, and having done all, to stand. Stand therefore, having girded your waist with *truth*, having put on the breastplate of *righteousness*, and having shod your feet with the preparation of the *gospel of peace*; above all, taking the shield of *faith* with which you will be able to quench all the fiery darts of the wicked one. And take the helmet of *salvation*, and *the sword of the Spirit, which is the word of God.* (Ephesians 6:13–17)

I will never forget that day in the kitchen because that is the day the Holy Spirit gave me the name of my new ministry: "The centurion answered and said, Lord, I am not worthy that thou shouldest come under my roof: but *speak the word* only, and my servant shall be healed" (Matthew 8:8 KJV).

Speak The Word Ministries was birthed at that moment. I didn't know it at the time, but this book was birthed at that moment, too. More importantly, at that moment God saw you. He knew you would one day pick up this book and the sword He's given you for your battle would be sharpened by the sword He's given me for mine.

Please allow me to pray for you right now:

Prayer

Father, I ask You to strengthen my friend through the reading of this book and its teachings. Grant ~~him~~ her proficiency in exercising ~~his~~ her authority as Your child, a soldier of The Most High God. In Jesus' name, Amen.

Introduction

Our minds have been programmed by the world around us since our first day on earth. It begins with the voices of our parents and continues through the voices of family, friends, neighbors, teachers, church leaders, and so forth, not to mention the media—radio, television, movies, social media, and music. This programming produces a mindset which shapes the words we speak and the beliefs we hold in our hearts.

If our thoughts conform to the world's viewpoints, it will lead to death, sickness, poverty, and destruction. The god of this world is a thief named Satan, who wants to steal, kill, and destroy us.

What should we do?

Instead of being *con*formed, we should be *trans*formed: "And do not be conformed to this world, but be transformed by the renewing of your mind, that you may prove what is that good and acceptable and perfect will of God" (Romans 12:2).

It is God's desire to reprogram us through His written Word so we see things as He does. When our words and thoughts agree with God's Word, we will see victory instead of defeat, healing rather than sickness, prosperity instead of poverty, and total restoration in our lives.

Dear saint, renewing our minds is a process which takes time and effort on our part. It is not easy, but it is doable. Before we turn the page to Chapter One, please allow me to pray for you:

Prayer

Lord, I ask for clarity of heart and soul as my friend digests the words of this book. Let the words roll over in her spirit, until she can fully grasp what You are revealing in my friend's heart. In Jesus' name, Amen.

Chapter 1
Victory in Your Mouth

One morning about ten years ago, I sat on the sofa at my home in Mount Olive, North Carolina, drinking tea, praying, and spending time with the Lord. As I sat there, praising and worshipping the Lord, my body felt hot and began to itch.

The word *hot* hardly describes it, though. I was super-hot, like a fiery liquid had flooded my body. It bothered me so much I walked out the front door and stood outside for a few minutes to cool off. I began praying.

I went back inside, wondering what to do. Should I phone my sister and have her drive me to the emergency room?

All of a sudden, I decided to speak to it.

The Lord had been impressing on me for quite some time about speaking His word to my problems, but I was still in the early stages of this revelation. Even so, I spoke to my body heat and the itch.

After speaking, I confessed God's healing words over me and kept doing it. I went into the bathroom and looked in the mirror. I looked horrible! A red rash covered my face, neck, and arms. As far as I could see, the red rash covered my whole body.

This could not have happened at a more inconvenient time, because I was scheduled to work as a chaplain at the Duplin Correctional Center that day. I had to show up. *What am I going to do?* I wondered.

My next thought centered on trusting God. I had already prayed over my body, spoken to my body, and confessed God's Word over it. I decided to trust Him. I undressed and stepped into the shower.

God knows I can't sing, but I sang in the shower that morning. I sang every song I knew concerning the blood of Jesus. It may have been off key, but I did it with all of my heart: "There is power, power, wonder-working power in the blood of the Lamb. There is power, power, wonder-working power in the precious blood of the Lamb."

By the time I finished my shower, the rash had mostly disappeared from my body. I brushed my teeth, put on makeup, and praised God at the same time. When I looked again, the rash was gone. My face and body were all cleared up.

But . . . (There is always a *but*, right?)

Satan never stops attacking us with one visit. We must always be prepared for his counterattacks after our victories. We can be healed today, but tomorrow he may try to put it back on us again. He may try to make us think we weren't healed in the first place. That's a lie! We need to be wise to his schemes.

The rash came back two or three more times, but each attack was a little less severe than the first one. I spoke to it and it left every time.

"Put on your new nature, and be renewed as you learn to know your Creator and become like him" (Colossians 3:10 NLT). Like our Father, we are speaking spirits who can speak words of life to ourselves and to others. We have victory in our mouths.

Voice-Activated Blessings

It seems as if everything is voice-activated in our modern world. We can text and call people simply by speaking to our phones. Televisions, cars, wristwatches, and security systems also respond to our voices. Who knows what new technology will next improve our lives using our voices?

Did you know that God's blessings are voice-activated, too?

It's not that God has reinvented Himself or His ways to fit into our world today; God has not changed. He's the same yesterday, today, and forever.[1] Yet the Bible reveals how we can gain victories and live victorious lives by filling our mouths with His Words and speaking them forth:

> The heart of the wise teaches his mouth, and adds learning to his lips. (Proverbs 16:23)

> This Book of the Law shall not depart from your mouth, but you shall meditate in it day and night, that you may observe to do according to all that is written in it. For then you will make your way prosperous, and then you will have good success. (Joshua 1:8)

Why aren't all believers living victorious lives? I believe the first place to look for an answer to that question is our mouths. Are we still proclaiming His Word? Has His Word departed from our mouths?

Hotel maids and maintenance workers have passkeys for opening room doors to do their work. It saves them time and energy to carry just one key rather than one for each door. God has done the same for us by making our tongues like passkeys, ones that will unlock all of the doors to healing, finances, promotions—whatever we need to live victorious lives in the kingdom of God.

Words set us apart. They make us special and unique, distinct from the animals. With our words we can communicate with other people on various subjects, but more importantly, we can speak to God and speak like Him to our situations and over our lives.

"Death and life are in the power of the tongue, and those who love it will eat its fruit" (Proverbs 18:21). Words have the power to give life to something or to kill it. A sobering truth, right? Our victories reside as words in our mouths, but so do our defeats. It will always be one or the other; there is no neutral ground with our tongues.

1. Hebrews 13:8

THE WEAPONS OF A WARRIOR

"And since we have the same spirit of faith, according to what is written, 'I believed and therefore I spoke,' we also believe and therefore speak" (2 Corinthians 4:13). God gave us mouths to change the seasons of our lives, change our circumstances, and turn our ships around when we're sailing in the wrong direction. He gave us mouths to praise Him and to speak creative blessings from His Word into existence, just like He did when He first framed the universe and everything in it with His words.[2]

> In the beginning [before all time] was the Word (Christ), and the Word was with God, and the Word was God Himself. In Him was life [and the power to bestow life], and the life was the Light of men. (John 1:1, 4 AMP)

> I will worship toward thy holy temple, and praise thy name for thy lovingkindness and for thy truth: for thou hast magnified thy word above all thy name. (Psalm 138:2 KJV)

God and His Word are one and the same. Thus, when we are speaking His Word, we're speaking Him forth. We need to pause and reflect on this truth. It will bless our lives when it becomes a lasting revelation for each of us.

In fact, God is so serious about the words we speak that on the Day of Judgment, we will give an account for every idle—nonworking, empty, careless, and inoperative—word we speak.[3] If God says every idle word will be examined by Him, He means just that! Maybe if we examine our words now, it will save us problems later.

Each believer is created in God's image as a speaking spirit.[4] We have the power, like our heavenly Father, to call forth things that do not now exist as though they do by faith and then see them come

---

2. Hebrews 11:3
3. Matthew 12:36
4. Genesis 2:7 (Aramaic Translation)

forth in God's timing.[5] We can do this with Christ's wisdom: "For assuredly, I say to you, whoever says to this mountain, 'Be removed and be cast into the sea,' and does not doubt in his heart, but believes that those things he says will be done, he will have whatever he says" (Mark 11:23).

I remember the time my dishwasher broke down. David picked up the phone and began phoning repairmen. But I thought, *God made everything, even this machine.*[6] *If He made it, then I can speak to it.* I laid hands on the dishwasher and spoke to it. "Lord, You said You made everything. If You made it, I can speak to it. So, dishwasher, I speak to you and I command you to work in Jesus' name."

The dishwasher began working. I asked David to cancel the repairman, which he was glad to do.

I spoke to my palm trees and plants when they looked dead, too. The gardeners told me to replace them, but after I spoke to the trees and plants, they revived and came back to life. I still talk to my plants today. Just so you know, they're looking great.

Maybe you think I'm crazy, but here's my thinking: if the Lord has given us permission to speak to something, it's up to us to do it. It's not up to Him, but it's up to us. He is not going to come down from heaven and speak to the mountains in our lives for us. We have to speak to them. We have to do our part and He will do His part.

Declarations and Decrees

"Put on your new nature, created to be like God—truly righteous and holy" (Ephesians 4:24 NLT). Our new nature is to talk and act like our Father. This means we can declare truths over our lives. Also, since we are heirs of God and joint heirs with Christ, we can speak decrees, like a king or ruler does to his subjects.[7]

---

5. Romans 4:17
6. John 1:3
7. Romans 8:17

For example, the Word states all things are possible with God.[8] Thus, we could say, "I declare, decree, and affirm with absolute faith from this day forward that I believe all things are possible through His anointing upon me and His Word, recognizing God as my source."

Here's another example: I declare with absolute faith that through God's anointing I shall not have want or lack, experience poverty, or suffer need. I shall be supplied with all of God's blessings, both natural and spiritual, to fulfill my destiny. I declare that I shall attract God's abundance in all forms. I decree that whatever I set my hands to touch will prosper and succeed because God's favor brings promotions and increase to my life.

I declare that everything the devil has stolen from me, he has to return to me seven times over because I have His favor and am a child of the Most High God and also because it says so in His Word: "People do not despise a thief if he steals to satisfy himself when he is starving. Yet when he is found, he must restore sevenfold; he may have to give up all the substance of his house" (Proverbs 6:30–31).

I'm a living witness to the truth of the above verses. Satan stole my husband (through an early death), my house, and my finances; he even tried to kill me, but the Lord whispered the above verses to my heart. He told me to stand on them and demand the thief restore sevenfold to me.

If we're standing on the Word, how long do we have to stand?[9] We stand until it appears in our lives and we can touch it. In my case, some of it was restored to me in a few days, some took weeks, others months, and a few took years, but I got it all back. Not seven times over, but a hundred times over—and I'm still getting back more today.

If we can identify the thief, he has to give it back to us. This is His Word. We can trust and stand on it.

"Put Me in remembrance; let us contend together; state your case, that you may be acquitted" (Isaiah 43:26). We have a part to play in

8. Matthew 19:26
9. Ephesians 6:13

this restoration because we must put Him in remembrance of His Word. In this instance, I wrote everything down and outlined what Satan took from me. Then, I outlined and asked what I wanted back. *[Hfw]* I am specific when I pray.

If I want a house on the beach, I ask for a house on the beach. If I want a new Chevrolet, I ask for a new Chevrolet. If I want my right leg to be healed, I ask for my right leg to be healed. I am specific and feel all believers should be specific in their prayers because we are going to receive what we ask for, right?[10] *I want children who passionately love to serve the Lord.*

Have you ever noticed how God always gives you more than you asked? Do you realize that every kernel of corn planted in the ground produces far more than one kernel? A kernel usually produces a stalk with two ears. Each ear has an average of 800 kernels. So, one kernel returns sixteen hundred times as much.

Sevenfold represents full, complete, and perfect payback. Hallelujah! "Oh, fear the Lord, you His saints! There is no want to those who fear Him. The young lions lack and suffer hunger; but those who seek the Lord shall not lack any good thing" (Psalm 34:9–10).

The Power of Words

From the Book of Genesis to the Book of Revelation, the Scriptures reveal the power in speaking and agreeing with His Word. Yet, there is also power in speaking words not agreeing with God, too.

> At one time all the people of the world spoke the same language and used the same words. As the people migrated to the east, they found a plain in the land of Babylonia and settled there.

> They began saying to each other, "Let's make bricks and harden them with fire." (In this region bricks were used instead of stone, and tar was used for mortar.) Then they said, "Come, let's build a great city for ourselves with a tower that reaches into the sky. This

---

10. Mark 11:24

will make us famous and keep us from being scattered all over the world."

But the Lord came down to look at the city and the tower the people were building. "Look!" he said. "The people are united, and they all speak the same language. After this, nothing they set out to do will be impossible for them! Come, let's go down and confuse the people with different languages. Then they won't be able to understand each other."

In that way, the Lord scattered them all over the world, and they stopped building the city. That is why the city was called Babel, because that is where the Lord confused the people with different languages. In this way he scattered them all over the world. (Genesis 11:1–9 NLT)

Listen, my friend, God said that because the people were united and all spoke the same words, nothing would be impossible for them. Nothing! They would not need God to help them in their lives! They would succeed apart from their Creator!

Thus, God came down from heaven and confused the people with different languages so they couldn't understand and walk in agreement with each other. God created mankind to need a relationship with Him.

If only the church would understand this revelation, we'd see a powerful move of His Spirit.

One of our biggest problems today is that our churches are not speaking the same language. Because of this, Satan and his kingdom of darkness are eating us for breakfast, lunch, and dinner. We must speak the same language. It doesn't matter if we're Methodists, Baptists, Pentecostals, or whatever, we must get on the same page in order to see a revival in our nation. After all, it was man who started denominations, not God. We must quit talking about us and focus ourselves totally on Him. It must be all about Him.

"Again I say to you that if two of you agree on earth concerning anything that they ask, it will be done for them by My Father in heaven" (Matthew 18:19). The power of agreement by believers ends up with our Father working with us and for us. Anything we ask. Hallelujah! Agreement brings us into unity with the Father. Unlike the tower of Babel, the people in Babylonia—even though they were also in unity—had the Father working against them. They ended up being defeated because our words must agree with His Word.

Our words carry an awful lot of power, more than we probably realize.

God told Abraham He was going to make him a father of many nations.[11] Nothing is impossible for God because He can make things like this happen through His power. All Abraham had to do was come into agreement with God's Words about him. When Abraham did that, God made it happen. Today, Abraham is considered a "father of faith" because he believed God's words about him.[12] God can make it happen for us, just as He did for Abraham.

I believe the enemy has so programmed the minds of God's children that we no longer resist Satan, but instead, we have rolled over like little puppies and befriended him. We even talk Satan's language. The only reason to do this is to earn his favor, right? He has tricked us into doing what he wants rather than what God wants because Satan is clever and subtle.

My dad was a heavy drinker when I was growing up. We all wanted him to quit, but he told us that if he ever saw the devil on the bottom of a bottle of booze, he would stop drinking.

Well, the other children and I got a can of Red Devil Lye. It had a picture of a red-horned devil with a pitchfork on it. We cut the picture off the can and pasted it under a bottle of booze, but it didn't work. Dad didn't stop drinking.

11. Genesis 17:5
12. Romans 4:16

Of course, Satan doesn't come in the form of a red devil with a pitchfork. That's too obvious! He's subtler than that.

He comes with a little sip here and little sip there. A man peeks at a woman. The next thing you know, he will be saying, "I don't know what happened. I just fell out of love and fell into love again."

Things like this don't just happen. It's the result of a sneaky enemy who whispers in our ears. Then we think it's our own idea, but it's not; it's from Satan. His goal is to break up families and destroy lives.

The good news is that my dad eventually became a new person in Christ later in his life. Praise God, it's never too late for Him.

Think about the man who was hanging on the cross next to Jesus, one of the two thieves. He went to be with the Lord on that same day.[13] Salvation can happen on our deathbeds, but it's better to give our lives to Him earlier so we can enjoy walking with Him on earth.

I was a late bloomer myself, but I don't fret about it anymore. At first, I did. I thought about what I could have been doing for God all those years I wandered around in the world. But God always knows the day and time we will accept His love as a free gift for ourselves. So, we should never beat ourselves up because He loves us and is proud of us.

Be Imitators of God

"Therefore be imitators of God as dear children" (Ephesians 5:1). How do little children imitate their fathers? They dress up in their dads' clothing, shoes, hats, wear his colognes, ties, sip coffee from their cups, and do whatever they can to be like them.

But let's be honest—we don't know how God dresses. Does He wear a robe or a hat? Does He have sandals on His feet? Does He drink coffee? We have no clue about anything like that. We only know Him through His Word.

---

13. Luke 23:43

Thus, the only way we can possibly imitate Him is to speak His words and believe for the same results. His words create life and have fixed purposes when they are spoken.

We must train ourselves to speak God's Word, but it takes effort on our parts because it does not come naturally. It's easier and more natural to speak what we see and feel in our emotions. Like many spiritual things, it takes time to train our mouths.

"And be not conformed to this world: but be ye transformed by the renewing of your mind, that ye may prove what is that good, and acceptable, and perfect, will of God" (Romans 12:2 KJV). God knew we couldn't change ourselves until we changed the way we think. We need to think it, speak it, and act on it.

Jesus said He only did what he saw His Father doing and only said what He heard His Father say.[14] Jesus is our role model. We must follow His example and do the same.

Charles Capps, an evangelist and author who has gone home to be with the Lord, said one night when he was teaching on Mark 11:23 that the Lord spoke to him: "I have told My people they can have what they say, but they keep saying what they have."

This is a simple and profound truth.

Too many of us talk about our problems, instead of speaking His Word to our problems. You see, in order for us to have our lives and circumstances turned around, we need to stop speaking the way it is right now, and start speaking the way we want it to be according to His Word. We need to be like Abraham, calling into existence things that don't exist so that they come into being in our lives.[15] We can do this with Christ's wisdom.

Remember: as long as we say what we have, we will only end up with what we have and not what we want. God's Word only produces what we say.

14. John 5:19
15. Romans 4:17

THE WEAPONS OF A WARRIOR

"Now the parable is this: The seed is the word of God" (Luke 8:11). Jesus explained in this parable that the kingdom of God works like planting seeds. His Word is a seed. If we speak what we see in the natural, we will get more of the same. But if we want something different, we must speak something different.

Look beyond what you see. Look into God's Word because it is filled with unseen life, waiting to produce a harvest in our lives. We need to monitor the words coming out of our mouths.

God likens our hearts to types of soil.[16] It will grow whatever seeds we plant in it. The soil does not determine what grows in it, but instead we determine what the soil grows by our choices, just like farmers planting seeds.

When we put His Word in our hearts, that is what will grow. But if we put other stuff in there, that will also grow and mature. Many speak God's word as a seed today and then try to dig it up tomorrow with their negative words. Don't do that!

The words in the Bible sometimes look lifeless to us, but we need to remember that every word is filled with power. A bag of seeds may look lifeless, too. Then, when we plant them and add water, the seeds come to life. This is the exact same way God's Words work in our hearts when we speak them.

Do you realize a mustard seed can lie dormant for sixty years? Then, if light and water are added, the mustard seed will grow to be one of the largest shrubs in the garden. Jesus compared the mustard seed to our faith.[17]

Now, think of all the dreams and visions that are lying dormant inside each of us. These are like the mustard seeds, waiting for us to plant them. But if we don't plant them with our mouths, they won't blossom and mature. They will be without life and power.

---

16. Mark 4:14–20
17. Matthew 17:20

PASTOR JOANNE RAMSAY

Jesus said His words are spirit and life.[18] Since this is true, decree and declare God's Word aloud because faith comes from hearing and hearing by the Word of God.[19] Listen to others speak the Word, too. But the biggest harvests of blessings will come in our lives with us speaking His Word to ourselves. We activate His Word with our mouths.

Let me remind you: seeds don't grow by resting in a bag on a shelf. The same is true with His Word. We must speak them on a consistent basis.

God's Whispering

I once lived in a little town that my husband called Pickletown, North Carolina. The biggest business was Mount Olive Pickle Company on the corner of Cucumber and Vine Streets. There were two stop lights in the whole town. I had a ministry and was working hard at it, but the whole time, the Lord was constantly whispering new things in my spirit. I referred to these thoughts and ideas as nuggets. I wrote them down, confessed them aloud, and stood by faith, believing them.

You can never know how foolish I felt sitting on a sofa in Mount Olive, North Carolina confessing the things He put in my spirit. But everything from being on the radio (when I didn't know how to record anything) to the ministry I have today came from those nuggets spoken to me by God. Even my new husband.

Although I didn't think I needed one, God knew I needed a husband. At the time, I was just happy doing God's work and running the race He placed before me. Yet, when God began whispering nuggets to my spirit about a husband, I wrote them down. You see, I was a widow for seven years before meeting my new husband.

---

18. John 6:63
19. Romans 10:17

THE WEAPONS OF A WARRIOR

I wrote down the verse He gave me about Boaz and Ruth. Then I told God I wanted a man after God's own heart like David.[20] I was specific and ended up with a man named David.

"Yes, again and again they tempted God, and limited the Holy One of Israel" (Psalm 78:41). Don't put limitations on God. We tie His hands when we do that. He won't be able to take us further in our walks with Him if we do that.

My prayer: Lord, I take the limitations off of You. Just do what You want to do, take me where You want to take me, but give me the courage to step through the doors You open for me.

No one expects the seed to come up the same day it's planted. We can't go out tomorrow and eat peaches from the seeds we planted today. "Night and day, while he's asleep or awake, the seed sprouts and grows, but he does not understand how it happens" (Mark 4:27 NLT). Like seeds, His Word planted in our hearts grows night and day. We don't necessarily understand the whole process, but we must have faith that the seeds are growing.

Would you like to see your mountains come down? You will as soon as you realize where the real battle is and who our real enemy is and that the battleground is in our minds. "For as he thinks in his heart, so is he" (Proverbs 23:7).

It's not our enemies. It's not the gossipers. It's not the liars, not our bosses, not our mates. It's none of these. "We're not waging war against enemies of flesh and blood alone. No, this fight is against tyrants, against authorities, against supernatural powers and demon princes that slither in the darkness of this world, and against wicked spiritual armies that lurk about in heavenly places" (Ephesians 6:12 The Voice). This is why we need to be covered head to toe with the full armor of God because our enemy is organized and persistent.[21]

So don't waste your energy on what people say about you. None of their words are holding us back from where we want to be in our

20. Acts 13:22
21. Ephesians 6:11

lives. Our problem is with what we've been speaking to ourselves, with the words we've planted in the soil of our hearts. Our words can keep the mountains up in our lives. "Your own mouth condemns you, not I. Your own lips testify against you" (Job 15:6 NLT).

We can release the power of God by the words of our mouths and cause His Word and His power to be available to us. Jesus used the written word and He must be our role model: "And the devil said unto him, If thou be the Son of God, command this stone that it be made bread. And Jesus answered him, saying, It is written, That man shall not live by bread alone, but by every word of God" (Luke 4:3–4 KJV).

Let's no longer let the words of our mouths keep us in bondage. Let's stop allowing Satan to defeat us with our own words. Let's not give the devil a foothold into our lives. Our feet belong to God and they are shod with peace! Our boots are spit-shined army style and we are ready to march!

Let's use our mouths for what they were created to do: praise God and declare His Word.

After he sinned, Adam hid from God and offered a lame excuse about being naked. God said, "Who told you that you were naked?"[22]

God wanted to know who Adam had been talking to. The same is true when we think there is no cure for a disease. Or no power in God anymore. Or no miracles because they stopped when the apostles died. Or we can't be promoted in our jobs. Or our debts are too big for God to help us. Who told us these things?

We're supposed to be imitating our Father and speaking His words. These words don't sound like anything God would speak to us. He speaks words of encouragement. If God did not say it, then it must have been Satan and you know it has to be a lie.[23]

Everyone is always so concerned about what other people say about them. It doesn't matter what they or the devil say. It only matters what we say. It's always, always, always what we say that will defeat us.

---

22. Genesis 3:11
23. John 8:44

21

"So the Lord said to him, 'Who has made man's mouth? Or who makes the mute, the deaf, the seeing, or the blind? Have not I, the Lord? Now therefore, go, and I will be with your mouth and teach you what you shall say'" (Exodus 4:11–12). Did God make our mouths, too? Is He able to teach us while we walk with Him?

The Word of God is the ultimate authority for us. We can declare, "Satan, you have no authority here or over me."[24]

It's time to believe and act on God's Word. When we do, we will become mighty in our circumstances. We will be the overcomer He says we are in Christ.[25]

Remember: tomorrow is a new day. Begin it the right way by decreeing and declaring His Word over your life.

Prayer

Father, as You were with David, be with my friend. Put a guard over her mouth and bridle on her tongue lest he should sin against You.[26] Help her to understand she must sow the seed in the soil of her heart to receive a harvest of blessings from You. In Jesus' name, Amen.

24. Luke 10:19
25. Romans 8:37
26. Psalm 141:3

Chapter 2

At Your Word

I f God said it, then I'm going to believe it without any *ifs* or *buts*." This should be our mindset when we read God's Word. Then we must act on it.

Keep in mind that our God is active and alert to perform His Word and His angels are standing by to carry out His plans, obeying His Word.[27] With this working for us, following His Word will always produce results for us.

We also must not look at other people's experiences and expect the same outcomes for ourselves. God does not work the same way each time in every believer's life. Our guide must always be His Word.

> Now when Jesus had entered Capernaum, a centurion came to Him, pleading with Him, saying, "Lord, my servant is lying at home paralyzed, dreadfully tormented."
>
> And Jesus said to him, "I will come and heal him." (Matthew 8:5–7)

The centurion answered:

> "Lord, I am not worthy to have You come into my home. Just say the word [speak the word, KJV] from where You are, and my servant will be healed." (Matthew 8:8 NLT)

27. Jeremiah 1:12; Psalm 138:2

THE WEAPONS OF A WARRIOR

This is the scripture the Lord gave me for the name of my new ministry a few years ago: Speak the Word Ministries. Hallelujah!

The centurion understood authority. He was used to speaking and giving orders to a hundred soldiers. When he spoke, he expected men to do exactly as he commanded them.

Now, I understand this officer's thinking because I have been around the military. I know that when an officer speaks, soldiers don't ask questions. They just do as they're told. As Christian soldiers we also need to listen to God's voice. If He says jump, we need to say, "How high, Lord?"

The centurion said, "I know this because I am under the authority of my superior officers, and I have authority over my soldiers. I only need to say, 'Go,' and they go, or 'Come,' and they come. And if I say to my slaves, 'Do this,' they do it" (Matthew 8:9 NLT). Jesus was amazed at the centurion's words. He had not seen faith like it in all of Israel.

Let's stop here for a moment.

Jesus was amazed a few times in the Gospels. He was amazed here with the centurion's faith, but He was also amazed twice with His disciples' lack of faith—once when He slept on a boat in a storm and another time when His disciples could not cast out a demon.[28]

Let's always try to amaze the Lord with our faith, OK?

"Then Jesus said to the Roman officer, 'Go back home. Because you believed, it has happened.' And the young servant was healed that same hour" (Matthew 8:13 NLT). Let's keep speaking His word to our problems. Let's keep believing for miracles and breakthroughs in our lives. Let's not settle for less than His best in everything we do.

> One day as Jesus was preaching on the shore of the Sea of Galilee, great crowds pressed in on Him to listen to the word of God. He noticed two empty boats at the water's edge, for the fishermen had left them and were washing their nets. Stepping into one of the boats, Jesus asked Simon, its owner,

---

28. Matthew 8:26; Matthew 17:17

to push it out into the water. So he sat in the boat and taught the crowds from there. (Luke 5:1–3 NLT)

Peter was tired from his long night of fishing on the Sea of Galilee, but still, he agreed to Jesus sitting in his boat and teaching the crowds of people. It had to be an effort on Peter's part to obey Jesus' instructions.

When he had finished speaking, Jesus said to Simon, "Now go out where it is deeper, and let down your nets to catch some fish." (Luke 5:4 NLT)

If only we had a video of Peter's facial expressions when Jesus spoke His words to him, but of course, we don't. We have to hear his weariness in his answer:

"Master," Simon replied, "we worked hard all last night and didn't catch a thing. But if You say so, I'll let the nets down again." (Luke 5:5 NLT)

The New King James Version states: "At Your Word I will let down the nets."

And this time their nets were so full of fish they began to tear! (Luke 5:6 NLT)

They caught so many fish that Peter and his crew had to shout to their partners in the other boat to come help them. Soon both boats were filled with fish and on the verge of sinking. Hallelujah!

When Simon Peter realized what had happened, he fell to his knees before Jesus and said, "Oh, Lord, please leave me—I'm such a sinful man." (Luke 5:8 NLT)

Peter was awestruck by the number of fish they had caught. So was his crew. His business partners, James and John, the sons of Zebedee, were also amazed at the miraculous fishing catch.[29]

---

29. Luke 5:10

Jesus replied to Simon, "Don't be afraid. From now on you will be fishing for people." (Luke 5:10 NLT)

As soon as they landed on shore, they left everything and followed Jesus.[30]

I think Peter's response revealed his feeling of insignificance in comparison to Jesus' greatness. I think he was awestruck.

Awestruck by God

You know, Peter had seen Jesus heal tons of people: the Bible says our Lord went about healing all that were afflicted and casting out demons.[31] Later, Peter saw Jesus raise the dead with His Word: "Now when He had said these things, He cried with a loud voice, 'Lazarus, come forth!' (John 11:43). Jesus didn't pray a long prayer. He spoke and a dead man heard His voice, got up, and walked out of a tomb. At His Word, Lazarus came back to life. Praise God!

Peter witnessed some breathtaking miracles by Jesus, but I believe he was first awestruck that Jesus cared about his day-to-day activities. It was this seemingly insignificant miracle with the fish—compared to the others—which showed Peter how much Jesus cared about him as a person.

I know we've probably all had times when we have been awestruck by what the Lord has done for us, where we've been totally amazed by His goodness. Maybe we've had miracles that helped pave our ways through rough times.

It's always good to pause and reflect on these moments where God leaves us speechless, and to remember them. Then we can draw on these memories when we have tougher days in the future.

One of my awestruck experiences occurred a month or so after my first husband passed away. I was dealing with grief and receiving hospital bills every day before then. My breakfast table was covered with bills, one of them for nearly $100,000. Even now, I can close my eyes and picture that table loaded down with hospital bills.

30. Luke 5:11
31. Matthew 4:23–24

26

You know, I teach people to lay hands on their bills, to lay hands on everything, to speak to this, to speak to that—and that is just what I did. I prayed over the bills, but I had not seen any results from my prayers.

Sometimes we pray and don't get any results right away. It's easy for us to start thinking that God didn't hear our prayers, isn't it? Well, this is where I was that day. I had no clear idea what I was going to do because more bills were coming in and I didn't know how much money I would have left to live on.

Then a desperate friend stopped by to see me. She needed to borrow money and wondered if I could loan it to her.

I laugh now, thinking about this experience, because I realize God had set me up. Did you know that the Lord sometimes does things like this to test us? He is checking our obedience.

At His Word is when the little soft voice inside you speaks and tells you to do something you don't feel you can or want to do. But whether or not we realize it at the time, our Father is really looking out for us. He has us covered.

My friend needed a loan, which seemed like a huge amount to me back then. She said she could pay me back in a few weeks. The problem was, I had no idea how much money I had to spare, because not all the receipts and bills had come in yet.

Still, I really felt in my spirit that I should loan her the money, so I did. If I remember correctly, this occurred on a Wednesday or Thursday.

The following Sunday afternoon I sat in my living room, working on my Sunday night message. The Lord interrupted my studying by speaking to me. He told me to go back and pray over the medical bills again, using a specific verse, 2 Kings 4:1, when I prayed.

My first thought was, "Lord, I have prayed already."

But at His Word I wrote down the words He impressed upon my spirit. I went and laid hands on the bills again and prayed over them.

Next He told me to call my friend and tell her that her debt had been canceled. She owed me nothing. I said, "Okay, Lord."

THE WEAPONS OF A WARRIOR

At His Word I went and called her. She wasn't there so I left a message, telling her she owed me nothing. Her debt was paid in full.

This took place on a Sunday.

When the mailman came the next day, I happened to be outside, sweeping the driveway. He drove up the driveway and handed me my mail, which I think was the first time he ever had done that. The mailbox was at the front of the house, and since I lived on a corner lot, the driveway was on the side of the house, so it really was an odd thing for him to hand me my mail in my driveway.

There was another medical bill in my mail. I opened it and saw that the almost $100,000 debt had been reduced to a figure of a little over $200. Praise God!

A month later this $200 debt was paid in full. The huge debt was paid off.

We need to realize that there were some things I had to do, even though I had already prayed over the bills. It sort of reminds me of Peter when he said, "Lord I fished all night and my nets are empty. I didn't catch a thing."

Jesus said, "Well, go cast them again."

Peter replied, "At Your Word Lord, I'll do it."

So when the Lord told me to pray over those bills again, I said, "Okay, Lord, I'll do it." At His Word, I prayed again. Hallelujah!

I was awestruck at the goodness of God and could barely talk. I thanked God and prayed in tongues. Words didn't seem adequate enough for me to let Him know how I felt about Him at that moment.

You know, we can all be a little awestruck when we've been praying for something and God answers our prayers. His goodness overwhelms us.

Sometimes God answers our prayers even before we ask Him. He will give us things that we might have been desiring, but had not bothered asking Him. When this happens, we are always awestruck by His goodness.

Here's something I've learned over the years: if I spend 99% of my time praising and thanking God *and* praying for other people's needs, then God will pour out His blessings on me. Most of the time I don't even have to ask. Thank you, Jesus!

Obedience

I was watching a movie about Queen Esther when the Lord began pointing out something important to me. Each time King Ahasuerus said something, a royal guard would answer, "At his Word, it shall be done," or sometimes, "By your words, it will be done."

This was when the Lord alerted me to the importance of these words.

You know, we can be watching a movie or listening to a song, and the Lord may choose to speak to us. It's His decision when and how He speaks. We just have to be tuned into hearing His voice.

I began thinking about the statement: *at His Word.*

What about Your word, Lord? If the servant in the movie would do what the king wanted him to do without questioning him, what about us? The royal guard always said, "At your word it shall be done," or "By your word it shall be done." It didn't matter what the king said because the royal guard's answer was the same. I think if the king had asked him to go climb Mount Everest, he would have said, "At your word."

Lord, this is so awesome, I thought.

How much greater is our Father's Word? How much more should we honor every word He speaks to us? In other words, if God's Word says we're prosperous, then we need to be speaking that out of our mouths— at His Word. If His Word says we are healed, that is what we should speak—at His Word. We need to speak and act on His Words.

We can listen to a doctor's or a banker's words, respect their positions and who they are, but we don't have to act on their words. We can leave their offices, walk outside, and declare, "Lord, that is not Your Word. That's not what You said to me."

The Lord can heal a person, even if a doctor has given up on him. The Lord can give a person what he needs, even if he has no credit and

THE WEAPONS OF A WARRIOR

bankers won't loan him any money. You know, He can even clean up credit scores overnight.

I'm not suggesting we go out and get bad reputations and then expect Him to clean up our messes; what I'm saying is, He has done it and He can do it for all of us.

The problem is, so many of us make silly messes and expect Him to clean them up right away. That's a different story! God will forgive and help us out of our messes, but we need to repent of the foolish things we've done. I've made some bad decisions, but I've repented of them. That's what we all need to do. We need to say, "Lord I was really ignorant about that. I didn't use any wisdom and forgot about asking for Your wisdom. Will You forgive me? I need Your help."

We have to have sincere and contrite hearts. We can't be thinking about making the same mistakes again and hoping the results will turn out differently next time. We need to act on God's Word. "If you diligently heed the voice of the Lord your God and do what is right in His sight, give ear to His commandments and keep all His statutes, I will put none of the diseases on you which I have brought on the Egyptians. For I am the Lord who heals you" (Exodus 15:26).

Jehovah Rapha means "the Lord who heals us." Even if the doctors and Satan tell us we're going to die, we can trust Jehovah Rapha—at His Word.

> Then Abraham lifted his eyes and looked, and there behind him was a ram caught in a thicket by its horns. So Abraham went and took the ram, and offered it up for a burnt offering instead of his son. And Abraham called the name of the place, The Lord Will Provide; as it is said to this day, "In the Mount of the Lord it shall be provided." (Genesis 22:13–14)

Jehovah Jireh means "the Lord who will provide for us." If Satan and everyone say that we will never get out of debt, we don't have to listen to them. We can listen to Jehovah Jireh—at His Word.

Our Father will supply all of our needs. He will supply our financial needs or any other needs that we may have. He is *El Shaddai*—the All Sufficient One, the Lord God Almighty.

El is a Hebrew name that is translated as *God* in the Old Testament. *Shaddai*, in the Hebrew, means "the breasted one." Therefore, El Shaddai refers to our God who completely nourishes and satisfies His people with all their needs as a mother would her child.

We need to think about what God says in His Word. We need to meditate on it and take him at His Word.

How many of us realize that He cares about every detail of our lives? There is nothing too small for Him to care about. "What is the price of five sparrows—two copper coins? Yet God does not forget a single one of them. And the very hairs on your head are all numbered. So don't be afraid; you are more valuable to God than a whole flock of sparrows" (Luke 12:6–7 NLT).

Did you know the copper coin was the smallest and least valuable coin in Palestine during Jesus' time? It was worth about six minutes of a worker's average day's wage. Yet, God cares about one sparrow that is worth less than one copper coin, and does not forget about it.

Jesus even said that our hairs are all numbered, not counted. If hair number 585 fell out of my head this morning, He knew it. There is nothing He does not know about us. So when Jesus said, "Don't be afraid," it's because God values us more than a whole flock of sparrows. He loves us and has His eye on us.

"I am in them and You are in Me. May they experience such perfect unity that the world will know that You sent Me and that You love them as much as You love Me" (John 17:23 NLT). God loves us as much as He loves Jesus. This may seem hard to believe sometimes, but it's true because He says it in His Word. Jesus is one with the Father and the Father is one with Him. We are one with Jesus and He is one with us. We are all one. And if that wasn't enough, He made each believer an heir and joint heir with Jesus.[32] Our life and legacy is tied to Jesus.

---

32. Romans 8:17

This proves how much He loves us and cares about every little detail in our lives.

But if He loves us so much, why are we having such a hard time? Why do we struggle in our finances? Why are we suffering from sickness? Why do we have rebellious children? Why do we not have peace in our homes?

Why? Why? Why?

We have to begin to establish His Word in all of our circumstances. We have to take Him at His Word. We have to begin to speak His Words. We have to begin to agree with God's Word. We need to speak God's Word when we're on our jobs. We need to speak God's Word when we're in our homes. We must speak God's Word over our children. It is our responsibility to speak His Words over every situation and circumstance confronting us on a daily basis.

"You have exalted above all else Your name and Your word and You have magnified Your word above all Your name!" (Psalm 138:2 AMP). If God has honored His Word so highly, we must do the same. And believe Him at His Word.

Prayer

Father, help my friend to take You at Your Word and to move when You whisper to her spirit. Grant her the grace and wisdom to act on whatever You tell her from this day forward. In Jesus' name, Amen.

Chapter 3
Faith Speaks

In 1996, my late husband and I lived in a beautiful home in Warsaw, North Carolina. He was the County Manager of Duplin County, which meant he supervised the managers of numerous departments and agencies, and worked with the elected Board of County Commissioners.

We hadn't lived there long when he decided to show appreciation for his fellow workers by holding a cookout for them and their families at our home. It rained all that week leading up to Saturday evening. The rain didn't dampen our enthusiasm, because our house was big enough to handle the crowd, but I wasn't satisfied with settling for a plan B.

I began praying and seeking the Lord.

Now, I admit to being a fairly new Christian at the time, having been saved just three years earlier, but I felt like testing my faith.

You know, I think sometimes it's easier for new Christians to exercise their faith than those who have years of experience. New believers aren't held back by past failures and aren't so set in their ways as those who have known the Lord for forty or fifty years.

My faith centered on the belief that if I prayed, God would hear me. "And if we know He hears us, whatever we ask, we know that we have the petitions that we have asked of Him" (1 John 5:15). I still believe that today because God hasn't changed.

My simple prayer was that God would hold back the rain on that Saturday evening so we could enjoy our cookout outside.

Saturday arrived along with another major rainstorm. It poured down. My husband and brother-in-law stood out by the garage, holding umbrellas and roasting a hog on the barbeque grill. I stayed the course, kept praying and thanking the Lord for holding back the rain for our cookout while handling preparations in the kitchen. Yet, the rain kept pouring down.

After a while, people arrived and questions were asked. "What are you going to do about the rain?"

I ignored their questions and kept doing what I knew to do, adding action to my faith. As I stirred potato salad, I kept praying and speaking to the Lord: "Thank you, Jesus, thank you, Lord, that you heard me when I prayed. Thank you, God, that the rain is going to stop. I don't know how it will happen, but I believe it will, even though it doesn't look like it will right now."

I also put the Lord in remembrance. "Lord, I'm not moved by what I see in the natural. I'm only moved by what the Word says. And the Word says if I pray and believe it's going to happen, it will happen."[33]

Ah, this is where the rubber meets the road—and where we can slide off into a ditch. It's easy to look at the dreary circumstances with our eyes and forget about God's Word and the One who backs up His Word. Nothing is impossible for Him!

Besides, who do you think speaks through our friends and other people when the circumstances look bad for us? The devil. When we are in the midst of one of our ugly situations, standing in faith and holding onto God's promises with all our heart, others may be trying to undermine us with their doubting words from the devil. Don't pay attention to them! Keep speaking the Word.

The people continued to arrive at our home that evening with more questions. "What are you going to do about the rain? Are you going to have it inside? What are you going to do? What are you going to do?"

33. Mark 11:24

34

Finally, I had my fill of questions. "No, this is a cookout, not a cook-in. We are going to hold it outside."

It was still pouring down rain and had been doing so for days. I couldn't argue with those facts, because there was no sign the weather was ever going to change. My proof was in the unseen. "Now faith is the substance of things hoped for, the evidence of things not seen" (Hebrews 11:1).

More people arrived, but as God is my witness, the rain ceased. We began setting up tables and chairs outside. "Aren't you afraid the rain will start again?" a few people asked.

"No, keep setting up tables. It'll be okay," I said.

Everyone sat at the tables under the trees in our yard, enjoying the cookout. All of this happened without any rain falling on us, but all around, the skies were black. It was raining everywhere, except in Warsaw, North Carolina, that evening.

As we finished eating, one of the commissioner's wives looked over at me. "Hey, Jo, look over there at that cloud," she said, pointing at the sky. "It looks like a hand holding back the rain."

In my spirit, I felt the Lord whisper, "Yes that's My hand. I'm holding back the rain."

We finished our dinner and gathered up the plates and dishes to take inside our home. The moment everything was inside, it started raining again. It rained for another two or three days.

There will be those who pooh-pooh this experience by saying, "Jo, that was just a coincidence."

No, it wasn't!

I prayed. I believed. I received a miracle.

All doubts should revolve around one question: is there a biblical example of a person praying about the weather?

The prophet Elijah prayed and then spoke to Ahab, King of Israel: "As the Lord God of Israel lives, before whom I stand, there shall not be dew nor rain these years, except at my word" (1 Kings 17:1).

God answered his prayer. It did not rain in Israel for three years until the prophet prayed again:

> Then it came to pass the seventh time, that he said, "There is a cloud, as small as a man's hand, rising out of the sea!" So he said, "Go up, say to Ahab, 'Prepare your chariot, and go down before the rain stops you.'" Now it happened in the meantime that the sky became black with clouds and wind, and there was a heavy rain. So Ahab rode away and went to Jezreel. (1 Kings 18:44–45)

I love what the New Testament says about Elijah's miraculous rain experience: "Elijah was as human as we are, and yet when he prayed earnestly that no rain would fall, none fell for three and a half years! Then, when he prayed again, the sky sent down rain and the earth began to yield its crops" (James 5:17, 18 NLT).

Some versions say Elijah was an "ordinary" man, much like you and me. So, if Elijah was just an ordinary person, we can have the same results with our prayers.

This experience occurred because I studied God's Word for myself. I made an effort to know Him, but my faith did not grow to this level overnight. It was a day-by-day process from when I first gave my life to the Lord in 1993.

Like every new believer, I started at the beginning with my measure of faith and moved forward from there.[34]

His Word Provides Answers

Our answers for overcoming life's circumstances are found in His Word. It doesn't matter what the problems might be, because His Word is sufficient to handle every one of them. We activate the power of His Word by speaking it. There are no shortcuts here. We must learn how to speak God's language to our mountains if we want them to fall down. Then God will act on our behalf.

---

34. Romans 12:3

"For the eyes of the LORD run to and fro throughout the whole earth, to show Himself strong on behalf of those whose heart is loyal to Him" (2 Chronicles 16:9). God is for us and never against us.[35] It's His desire to bless us, but we must keep our hearts loyal to Him. Once again, there are no shortcuts here, because we must imitate Him as little children do their fathers.[36]

> The LORD said to my Lord, "Sit at My right hand, till I make Your enemies Your footstool." (Psalm 110:1)

Jesus referred to the above verse in His teachings. He let us know He's willing to help us make our enemies our footstools. Are you hearing me? This means our problems will be under our feet and not hanging over our heads. He'll do this despite the economy or the money markets or our doctor's reports.

You know, the Lord revealed to me there is coming a shifting and transfer of wealth into the lives of His children. Hallelujah! "A good man leaves an inheritance to his children's children, but the wealth of the sinner is stored up for the righteous" (Proverbs 13:22).

My friend, we are the righteousness of God if we have given our lives to Christ.[37] This means the wealth of the sinner is stored up for us. I pray this happens for you and me. I need the finances to accomplish what God has called me to do. You need finances for your own vision, too. Yes, our source is God, but He supplies our financials needs through men and women. My prayer is this:

"Lord, I thank You for telling me there is coming a shifting and a transfer of wealth into the lives of Your children. I ask You to release Your angelic forces to gather it up and bring it into our storehouses. We can ask this because Your Word states that we are the righteousness of God in Christ Jesus. But even so, we're dependent on what Jesus did to make us righteous, not on our own righteousness. In Jesus' name, Amen."

---

35. Romans 8:31
36. Ephesians 5:1
37. 2 Corinthians 5:21

The Lord also told me that those who have been sitting in darkness shall come into the light. He spoke these words to me at the same time He talked about the transfer of wealth. You know, when He said these words about coming into the light, I assumed He was only talking about sinners. As you probably know, when we're born again, we are transferred out of the kingdom of darkness into the kingdom of His Son.[38] But as I waited upon Him, He revealed that not only was He talking about unbelievers coming to the light, but also His believers, who have sat in darkness concerning His Word and the power of His Word. Praise the Lord!

The blinders will be coming off our eyes so we will recognize the true power of His Word and how it is activated when we speak it forth.

We have to stop listening to the lies of Satan, who is the father of lies and never speaks the truth.[39] We have to stop listening to the world's opinion on everything. We need to tune these out because it interferes with our faith.

Media Interferes With Our Faith

Years ago, when I began my prison ministry, the Lord instructed me not to watch the news on television or read newspapers. He said it would interfere with my faith and the right kind of heart I needed for His work.

It's hard enough to keep our faith strong for something we can't see and believe God will do for us, but it's even harder when we are watching TV. The media is against everything we believe in. Their words may defile us and interfere with our faith. At the least, it will slow our faith down because we put ourselves in a double-minded position of listening to the world's ways and trying to believe God at the same time.[40] This seldom ends well for His children; it allows Satan an opportunity to put doubt and fear into our hearts.

---

38. Colossians 1:13
39. John 8:44
40. James 1:6–8

We need God's wisdom and discernment on what we watch on television. If we take just a moment to ask Him, we can expect a quick answer from Him.

But as I stated earlier, we must learn to speak God's words. We must stop speaking idle, non-working words out of our mouths.[41] We must get a handle on our mouths. They prevent our breakthroughs. Our victories or our defeats reside right under our noses—in our mouths. "Though I were righteous, my own mouth would condemn me; though I were blameless, it would prove me perverse" (Job 9:20).

It probably seems that all I talk about is our mouths. Yet, this is what I am anointed and called to do. My ministry's name is Speak the Word Ministries. I want you and everyone to receive the revelation of speaking God's word for yourselves.

If God framed the world with His Word and held everything together by His Word, we need a revelation of the power in His Word.[42] This is where our power lies. It's not in money or having things, but it's in speaking His word to our mountains and watching them collapse.

If we speak His Word in faith, we will have the same results Jesus spoke about in Mark 11:23: "For assuredly, I say to you, whoever says to this mountain, 'Be removed and be cast into the sea,' and does not doubt in his heart, but believes that those things he says will be done, he will have whatever he says. Therefore I say to you, whatever things you ask when you pray, believe that you receive them, and you will have them."

Jesus did not say we could just have one or two things, but He said we could have whatever we said. Let's not limit ourselves if God has not put limits on us.

The other side of the coin is that often when we believe for healing or for finances for ourselves, everything seems to get worse almost right away.[43] Nothing looks better at all. Our world seems to be flying apart.

---

41. Matthew 12:36
42. Hebrews 11:3
43. Mark 4:17

What do we do? "Stand therefore, having girded your waist with truth" (Ephesians 6:14).

His Word is the truth. We must continue speaking His Word even though everything seems to be coming against it. If we keep planting His Word with our mouths, we will eventually reap a harvest of blessings. It's up to us to stand and continue speaking His Word, no matter what it looks like to our natural eyes.

When we follow the Lord and speak His Word, we can expect that Satan will oppose us. Let's make up our minds ahead of time about His Word being more powerful than the darts of the evil one. Then we can lift up our shields of faith, wield the sword of the Spirit against Satan, and keep on trucking.[44] Hallelujah!

Lots of people want to label me as a speak-it-and-claim-it teacher. To be honest, I sure do speak it and claim it. But there is a lot more to it than just speaking and claiming it. You have to believe in your heart about what you're saying. "If you confess with your mouth the Lord Jesus and believe in your heart that God has raised Him from the dead, you will be saved" (Romans 10:17).

It doesn't matter whether we desire salvation, healing, or prosperity for ourselves, God's only criterion is that we have faith in the words we speak. We have to know the mountains are taken care of by our words. When this happens, the mountains will move out of our way.

"Catch us the foxes, the little foxes that spoil the vines, for our vines have tender grapes" (Song of Songs 2:15). It's always the little things that keep us from enjoying the blessings of God's kingdom. One of the sneakiest little foxes that hinder our faith walk is not always being truthful in what we say. [45]

Let's say that we tell a friend we're going to do something and then we don't do it. Maybe something came up and interrupted our plans. Maybe it wasn't even our fault. Yet, we have to arrive at the place where we have faith in what we say. If something like this does happen to us, we

---

44. Ephesians 6:16–17
45. Matthew 5:37

must quickly ask forgiveness with a sincere heart. There has to be value in our words to others and ourselves.

For example, let's say we tell someone we will meet the person at 7 p.m., but we show at 7:15 or 7:30. If there's a legitimate reason for being late, phone the person ahead of time.

A pastor friend of mine was always an hour late for our meetings. Finally, I confronted her and told her how being consistently late for a meeting was wrong. It disrespected and revealed lack of concern for the other person—not a godly attitude on her part.

This same pastor had believed God for all kinds of miracles for years and had received none of them. Why? One reason for it was this little fox of untruthfulness, and she continued in it.

We have to have faith in our hearts about the words we say, knowing that they are going to come to pass. If we don't believe our own words, it causes confusion in our hearts. We have to honor our words before we can have faith in His Word. If this is a problem for us, we need to reflect on our habits and change them.

My friend, doesn't this make sense?

We must clean up our act. It won't happen overnight, but God will help us. If we need to change, then let's repent and God will forgive us. He's a merciful God and His mercies are new every day.[46]

If the Holy Spirit brings something to your mind at any time, repent, ask forgiveness, and go on your way. Satan might try to make you feel guilty, but just tell him, "Hey, devil, you don't get a vote in this. I'm forgiven. I'm a child of the Most High God. There is no condemnation for us who are in Christ Jesus.[47] The law of the spirit of life in Christ Jesus has set me free from the law of sin and death.[48] So, you don't get a vote here."

Charles Capps went home to be with the Lord a few years ago, but his teaching ministry still continues today. Brother Capps once said that the

46. Lamentations 3:22–23
47. Romans 8:1
48. Romans 8:2

Lord spoke to him concerning confessing the Word of God aloud where you can hear yourself saying it.[49] He said the Lord told him that the Body of Christ must learn to live in the authority of His Word because God's Word has creative power in it.[50] This creative power is produced by the heart, formed by the tongue, and released out of our mouths in words. For the word to be effective, we must speak it in faith.

We have to quit saying, "Well I'm never going to get these bills paid off. Honey, we aren't ever going to make it. We can forget the vacation this year. We haven't paid for last year's vacation yet."

And stop saying, "I can't ever do anything right. I'm never going to get well. I'm going to have to live with this pain for the rest of my life."

People constantly tell me that their doctor could offer no medical cure for them; they were told they had to learn to live with their ailments. How many people have heard these same things?

We don't have to learn to live with afflictions or anything else. We have been given the power and authority to speak to any sickness in the name of Jesus. "That at the name of Jesus every knee should bow, of those in heaven, and of those on earth, and of those under the earth" (Philippians 2:10). Our sicknesses and every other affliction must bow its knee at the name of Jesus. Hallelujah!

Maybe our mama died from the same disease we're suffering from. This may be a fact, but His Word changes facts. We don't have to die like our mama did, because we have a new DNA—God's DNA. There is no sickness in His DNA. No sickness in heaven. He is our loving Father.

When I go to the doctor's office, I don't fill out the medical history part of the forms they want you to fill out. I don't tell them that stuff. I'm a new creation in Christ Jesus.[51] Why tell them about my past when it's under His blood?

49. Romans 10:17
50. Romans 4:12
51. 2 Corinthians 5:17

It doesn't matter if my brother or sister or my mother died of cancer. We are different people. Just so you know: my mama was a Christian and I sincerely loved her. So, I'm not putting her down by saying this. When she passed away, I wasn't even a Christian yet, but I do know mama wasn't taught about speaking His Word and walking in faith. Who knows what would have happened if she would have learned these truths?

To be honest, most people aren't taught what I'm writing right now. Therefore, we should be thankful to learn the truth and have it set us free.[52] It's God's truth that we need to hear. Do you agree with me?

Recently I woke up with pain and soreness in my back. I couldn't figure out where the pain and the soreness came from. When I went to bed, I wasn't sore or in pain. I was fine. So when I woke up that way, I began to reason in my mind, trying to figure out what had caused the pain and the soreness. I was on my way to take a Tylenol when I heard the voice of God say to me, "Why don't you speak to it?"

And I thought to myself, *Why don't I speak to it?* I said, "Lord, you are right. I'm going to speak to it."

He tells me that a lot.

So, I didn't take the Tylenol. I spoke to the pain and the soreness and soon they were gone. Hallelujah!

How many of us need a bigger revelation of our tongues, which hold the power of life and death in them?[53] I would raise my hand right away.

Some of us allow our tongues to control our whole lives. We let this little member say whatever it wants, not knowing the power of our words, not understanding what it is doing to us. We need to search God's Word, learn what it says, and then pray the answer. God is only going to bring to pass what His Word says He will do.

According to Mark 11:23, the Lord has given us the power and authority to speak to our mountains. Sometimes the mountain might be sickness in our bodies, but that doesn't matter because we have been given

---

52. John 8:32
53. Proverbs 18:21

the authority to speak to our bodies. We can speak to our kidneys, our lungs, our glands, our bones and joints. We can speak to any sickness— to a headache, to cancer, to diabetes. God has not placed limits on what we can speak to in His name. Hallelujah!

I'm learning more every day about how to exercise my God-given authority because I certainly have not arrived yet. I am still in school. This is a school where we all will attend until the day Jesus returns or takes us home. We are never going to learn it all here on earth. But let's keep at it.

When we are confessing God's Word over our situations and circumstances, His Word is going out into the spiritual realm and accomplishing what we are sending the words to do.

"So shall My word be that goes forth from My mouth; it shall not return to Me void, but it shall accomplish what I please, and it shall prosper in the thing for which I sent it" (Isaiah 55:11). His Word is not void of power but it is still working. His Word has not changed from the first day of creation until today.[54] Isn't it true that our Lord is the same yesterday, today and forever?[55] Well, then His Word is also the same yesterday, today and forever. It will never change. It is a spiritual law that we are going to get what we say. Hallelujah!

"'Is not My word like a fire?' says the LORD, 'And like a hammer that breaks the rock in pieces?'" (Jeremiah 23:29). Have you ever pictured God's Word as a hammer? When we speak His Word, it begins hammering away at our problems, breaking them into small pieces. It doesn't matter if the problem is a big rock or a tiny one. It's just that the bigger ones may take a little more hammering. Let's start hammering and keep at it.

We have to obey another spiritual law if we want success: "Out of the same mouth proceed blessing and cursing. My brethren, these things ought not to be so. Does a spring send forth fresh water and bitter from the same opening? Can a fig tree, my brethren, bear olives, or a grapevine bear figs? Thus no spring yields both salt water and fresh" (James 3:10–12).

---

54. John 1:1
55. Hebrews 13:8

We can't speak out of both sides of our mouths and expect miracles to happen. We have to speak His Word at our mountains and stop speaking the problems. If we do this, our mountains will be removed.

Prayer

Father, You said that the entrance of Your Word brings light. So, I ask You to send Your light and truth about Your Word into my friend's heart. Let it come alive with revelations for him from this day forward.

Chapter 4

The Authority
of the Believer

I put my home in North Carolina on the market a few years ago. Part of the sales process included having it checked out by a licensed termite inspector. The inspector discovered heavy termite damage; I had to hire a contractor to rip out half of my living room floor and replace it with new wood. The termites had done that much damage. Then I hired another contractor to deal with what the termites had done in other areas. It became quite expensive for me.

I'm not writing about termites here, but a bigger problem, one which many believers don't even consider: Satan. He is a lot like a termite that eats away at our lives as a thief and a destroyer.[56] Sadly, most of us aren't even aware that Satan and his demons are the thieves who cause many of our problems.

We have to learn how to fight Satan, because he's eating away at the foundations of our civilization. The only exterminators God has to stop this from happening are believers. We must learn how to exercise our God-given authority as soldiers in the war against the kingdom of darkness.

"But the Son of God came to destroy the works of the devil" (1 John 3:8 NLT). We are called to be like Jesus while we live in this world.[57] If He destroyed the works of the devil, then we are to do the same. There

---

56. John 10:10
57. 1 John 4:17

are no excuses for us not doing so because He has provided everything we need through His Word and His Spirit.

Think about this: you never see termites working, because they are always busy under the surface, causing damage in darkness. Satan also works in darkness.[58] We don't usually notice the devil until he has already done heavy damage in our lives.

In lots of ways, a termite is a paradox; you wouldn't think such a little thing could be so destructive. Yet, a colony of them are strong enough to eat a house, even though termites' bodies are soft and delicate.

I am a witness to the damage termites can cause. Our home in North Carolina, and later our guesthouse, needed to have two walls replaced because of termite damage. We didn't even know the guesthouse had a termite issue. It was only by accident we discovered the problem when we tried to hang a picture on the wall and couldn't do it. If the termites had continued unnoticed, the whole guesthouse would have collapsed.

Satan works the same way. If he is allowed to work unnoticed, we won't know we have a problem until it's too late. He is a master of deception. The Apostle Paul wrote that Satan can even disguise himself as an angel of light.[59]

So, what must we do?

Power to Live on Earth

When we gave our lives to Jesus Christ, He not only saved us, but also gave us power to live and rule here on earth. He died for our freedoms and gave His life so we could have more abundant lives for ourselves.[60]

> What are mere mortals that you should think about them, or a son of man that you should care for him? Yet you made them only a little lower than the angels and crowned them with glory and honor. (Hebrews 2:6–7)

Hallelujah! God has crowned us with glory and honor.

---

58. Colossians 1:13
59. 2 Corinthians 11:14
60. John 10:10

"You gave them authority over all things." Now when it says "all things," it means nothing is left out. (Hebrews 2:8 NLT)

God has given us authority over all things. The word "all" means "all," with nothing left out. There is no fine print in His Word because He says what He means!

Let's check out our God-given authority.

Number one: as believers we have authority and power over the devil.[61] This may not always seem true because the devil gives us such a hard time. Yet even when we get beat down, we always have the power to get right back up again.

Number two: the devil is subject to believers and has to obey us.[62]

Number three: the devil is subject to the Word of God.[63] He must obey God's Word; he has no other choice. It's like throwing darts at him when we speak God's Word. So, if we want to beat up the devil, spit out God's Word at him. It torments him.

And number four: the devil is subject to the believers' rights and can never take them away from us.[64] We might be deceived into thinking we have lost part of our believers' rights, but that is a lie!

Our main weapon is the Word of God, but that's more than enough to fight our way out of any battle with Satan.[65] We can stay on top and keep him under our feet. If we happen to trip and end up on the bottom, we can get right back up again. Speaking His Word will always put us back on top.

I don't know about you, but I don't always feel very spiritual. Sometimes, when I pray, my prayers feel cold and powerless. Sometimes, when I'm working on a teaching in my studio, I don't feel anything at all—nothing! But we need to keep in mind that our feelings don't matter. We can't base His presence in our lives by our feelings; we must

61. Luke 10:19
62. 1 John 4:17
63. Luke 4:4, 8, 12
64. John 10:28–30
65. Ephesians 6:17

base it on His Word. God's Word states He is with us always and will never leave us.[66]

"Faith takes God without any *ifs* added to it," said D. L. Moody. We must arrive at the point where if God said it in His Word, we will believe it without any *ifs* or *buts*, watering His Word down.

Not too long ago, I was telling the Lord, "God, I thank You that I don't have to base my salvation on my feelings. I thank You that my strength is not based on my feelings. I thank You that none of it is based on my feelings. I know You are here whether I feel Your presence or not."

"The human heart is the most deceitful of all things, and desperately wicked. Who really knows how bad it is?" (Jeremiah 17:9 NLT). If our hearts lie to us and can't be trusted, then we certainly can't trust our feelings. Let's always trust His Word over our feelings every time. It's the only way for us to be overcomers here on earth.

Praise Brings Victory

Here's something we need to keep in mind: singing. All through the Bible, songs have played a major role in worshipping God. Songs also reveal a glimpse of God's character and celebrate what He has already done in the world.

> The Lord is my strength and song, and He has become my salvation; He is my God, and I will praise Him; my father's God, and I will exalt Him. The Lord is a man of war; the Lord is His name. Who is like You, O Lord, among the gods? Who is like You, glorious in holiness, fearful in praises, doing wonders? You stretched out Your right hand; the earth swallowed them. (Exodus 15:2–3, 11–12)

I understand how the Israelites felt that day at the Red Sea because I've had plenty of times when I felt like I was between a rock and hard place and didn't know which way to go. I had my back against the wall, just as the Israelites did on that day when Pharaoh's army was heading straight at them and the Red Sea was behind them.

---

66. Hebrews 13:5

The Israelites felt trapped, but that wasn't the truth for them then, nor is it for us today. God has promised to always give us a way of escape.[67] All we have to do is ask Him.

The same Red Sea the Israelites walked through on dry land, without even getting their sandals muddy, became a watery grave for Pharaoh's army and chariots.[68] Hallelujah! Our God can turn defeat into victory with a wave of His right hand.

The Israelites rejoiced, praising and worshipping God in song because of what they saw that day, but we have a big advantage over the Israelites. We have His Word. In our deepest troubles and saddest moments, we can lift our hands to God and sing songs, declaring victory in every circumstance. We can keep on singing until we receive it. His Word backs up our songs of declarations. Hallelujah!

> And when King Jehoshaphat had consulted with the people, he appointed those who should sing to the Lord, and who should praise the beauty of holiness, as they went out before the army and were saying: "Praise the Lord, for His mercy endures forever."
>
> Now when Judah began to sing and to praise, the Lord set ambushes against the people of Ammon, Moab, and Mount Seir, who had come against Judah; and they were defeated. (2 Chronicles 20:21–22)

King Jehoshaphat and the army of Judah faced a larger and more powerful foe. They sought the Lord for His battle plan.[69] What did God have in mind? He told them to send out a praise and worship team before the army and watch Him fight the battle for them.

When soldiers go into battle, they often shout a war cry or voice a rhythmic chant as they march. This encourages them. But on this day, God didn't want Judah to see themselves as warriors. He didn't want to

---

67. 1 Corinthians 10:13
68. Exodus 14:21, 28
69. 2 Chronicles 20:4

hear their battle cries or chants. He was the Man of War, the Warrior who would fight for them.[70] He desired to hear their songs of praise.

At the moment Judah began to sing and praise Him, God ambushed the nation's enemies. Thousands of enemy soldiers turned and killed each other.[71] God caused it all to happen without Judah lifting one finger to help.

When the army of Judah finally arrived on the battlefield, all they saw were dead bodies lying everywhere. Not a single one of their enemies had escaped.[72] Hallelujah!

Not only that, King Jehoshaphat and the army of Judah ransacked their dead enemies of their valuables, precious jewelry, and clothing. It took them three days to gather all of the spoil because there was so much of it.[73]

Hallelujah! Isn't our God awesome?

Before the battle, God told Judah to not be afraid, to position themselves, to stand still and see the salvation of the Lord.[74] They followed His instructions and were blessed.

The Lord is telling us not be afraid of our enemies because He has overcome Satan for us.

Believers' Authority

Jesus sent seventy of His followers on a preaching and healing mission to the local cities.[75] When they returned, they were filled with excitement and said, "Lord, even the demons are subject to us in your name."[76]

Do you know how Jesus answered them? "I saw Satan fall like lightning from heaven" (Luke 10:18). When Jesus ushered in the kingdom of God,

---

70. Exodus 15:3
71. 2 Chronicles 20:23
72. 2 Chronicles 20:24
73. 2 Chronicles 20:25
74. 2 Chronicles 20:17
75. Luke 10:1
76. Luke 10:17

Satan's termination began that very moment. Satan is doomed. He is roaming around on the earth and is very much alive right now, but he still is doomed. Believers are now the overcomers.[77]

"Behold, I give you the authority to trample on serpents and scorpions, and over all the power of the enemy, and nothing shall by any means hurt you" (Luke 10:19). Jesus has given us authority over Satan and every demon, no matter how big or little. This was the authority man lost in the Garden of Eden when Adam and Eve listened to Satan.[78] Jesus got all of it back for us at the cross and His resurrection. Hallelujah!

"Those who see you [Satan] will gaze at you, and consider you, saying, "Is this the man who made the earth tremble, who shook kingdoms?"" (Isaiah 14:16). There's a day coming when we will be amazed at Satan, the one who caused us to walk in so much fear. We'll see him as a puny thing. Then we'll say, "Is this the one who kept me from getting my blessing? Is this the one who convinced me I couldn't succeed? Who stole my health and caused me so much pain? Who caused me to lose my money? Who took away my family?"

Hallelujah! There's good news for us!

We don't have to wait until Satan is thrown into the lake of fire because we can stop him from stealing from us right now. We aren't in the kingdom of darkness and one of Satan's subjects anymore.[79] We dwell in the kingdom of God and our King has given us authority over the devil.

Even better, we can get back whatever he has stolen from us: "Yet when the thief is found, he must restore sevenfold" (Proverbs 6:31). This is a part of our heritage as believers: a sevenfold blessing.

Back in 2003, Satan took my beach house after my husband passed away. It wasn't a big deal, just a mobile home on the beach, but it was a place where I enjoyed spending time with the Lord. My family enjoyed coming there and it was close to my ministry. I loved being near the ocean. Everything was fixed up and it no longer looked like a mobile home, but the devil stole it from me.

77. Romans 8:37
78. Genesis 3:6
79. Colossians 1:13

Our God, however, is always there for His children, waiting to help us. One day, the Lord brought Proverbs 6:31 to my attention. I wrote it down and began confessing the verse over my life. I want you to know the devil has given it back to me a hundred times over. Hallelujah!

Satan comes to steal, kill, and destroy us. This seems to be his fulltime job! It is up to us as children of God to stop him. If he does sneak in and get one over on us, then it's up to us to get it back.

Remember, God wants us to receive back what Satan has stolen from us, but He won't come down from heaven and do the work for us. It's up to each of us to do it for ourselves.

There are spiritual laws for healing and finances, which specify that we have to use His Word to get either back from Satan. We have been given authority and dominion by God over Satan, but it's up to us to believe this is true.

If we believe His Word is true, we can act on it, right?

Do we have to feel anything, like a special anointing, to do this? No. All we have to do is confess the Word of God over our lives and circumstances. This is our pathway to victory.

If Satan has us feeling bad enough, sad enough, and sorry enough for ourselves so we won't even confess His Word, Satan has us in his grip. Yet here's the good news: we can pray and ask the Lord for a verse. Write it down when He speaks it to you and then stand on it. It may take a day, week, month, or whatever, but we can still come out on top in the battle. Never give up!

We have to keep following Him. We've got to keep doing what He has called us to do. We have to keep serving others. If we're not serving people, then we're not serving Jesus. We must keep walking with the Lord, no matter what is happening in our lives. Our God will make sure we are taken care of if we are faithful to Him. It's as simple as that. Keep on marching.

Our believers' authority is not just for rebuking Satan, but also for knowing God is always on our side. Through His Word, we can stand in any storm. We can be the overcomers He has created us to be.

The Lord has told us we have authority and power over Satan and his demons. We need to accept that as fact and act on it. Our authority is not based on future promises, but is a statement of fact for today.

"And you shall know the truth, and the truth shall make you free" (John 8:32). The truth is that we are called to reign in life as kings and priests and not as victims of Satan and his lies.[80]

Pastor Darlene Bishop once told about a vision the Lord gave her. In it, He showed her the word "believe" as an acronym, standing for Because Emmanuel Lives, I Expect Victory Every time. B-E-L-I-E-V-E!

Hallelujah! That is something we should confess every day of our lives.

We should never expect defeat or consider going with a plan B. Don't make room for failure. Don't say, "If this doesn't work, we'll try that." Let's not set ourselves up for failure. Let's stick with God's plan.

"For whatever is born of God overcomes the world. And this is the victory that has overcome the world—our faith" (1 John 5:4). Jesus has already defeated Satan. He is a defeated foe. Let's get up in the morning and say, "Lord, because You live, I expect victory today. I thank you, Jesus, that Satan is a defeated foe and I have victory because of You."

Command Position of Authority

Which He worked in Christ when He raised Him from the dead and seated Him at His right hand in the heavenly places, far above all principality and power and might and dominion, and every name that is named, not only in this age but also in that which is to come. (Ephesians 1:20–21)

Jesus is seated at the right hand of the Father. He has authority over Satan and every level of the kingdom of darkness. That's good news for us, but continue reading.

"And [God] raised us up together, and made us sit in the heavenly places in Christ Jesus" (Ephesians 2:6). We have a joint seating with Jesus because we are united in Him. It's a position of authority. The church needs to believe

---

80. Revelation 5:10

His Word and believe all things are under our feet and Christ is the Head over all things.[81] When we do this, the church will see victory after victory.

Let's quit being so nice to Satan. Let's quit saying, "Dear devil, would you please leave me alone," or, "O Lord, I just wish the devil would stop bothering me today. Would you please take him off my back?" Instead, let's be proactive against Satan.

Why?

First of all, we should go on the offense because believers have been given authority and power to tread on Satan and all demons. The word "tread" means to trample upon, press, crush, or injure someone. In this case, it's the devil himself, but we must use His Word to do this.

Second, believers have been given the authority to speak to any situation or circumstance. We can speak to the areas of dry bones in our lives, but we need to expect something to happen when we speak His Word at our mountains. Otherwise, this is just a dead formula, which will not work for us. You see, God's Word is living and powerful and sharper than any two-edged sword.[82]

If we speak to a headache, a cut finger, or anything else, we must expect something to happen. It will, if we expect it to happen.

Third, believers have been given the power to command anything that comes against us. Command means a position of highest authority. Jesus Christ Himself has given us this high level of power and authority. Therefore, we can speak to our mountains in confidence, knowing they must obey our words.

The power is in His name and He gave us permission to use it: "Therefore God also has highly exalted Him and given Him the name which is above every name, that at the name of Jesus every knee should bow, of those in heaven, and of those on earth, and of those under the earth" (Philippians 2:9–10). His name causes demons to tremble. His name gives us access to the glory of God. His name moves mountains. His name opens doors to the blessings of God.

81. Ephesians 1:22
82. Hebrews 4:12

His name should thrill each of us when we hear it. "There's just something about His name," are the words of an old song, and they're still true today.

Let's Use Our Authority

Let's begin using the authority and power the Lord has given us. Let's speak to our mountains of sickness or fear or doubt. Let's speak to our mountains of debt or poverty. Let's expect something to happen because we have been given the highest level of authority from the Lord God Almighty.

It's hard for me to believe I used to take a hundred and fifty pills per month. One hundred and fifty pills! But I prayed and spoke His Word over my sickness. Today I'm healed. I have no sickness at all. Praise God! It was also through prayer and speaking His Word that I became debt free and able to be a blessing to others. So, my friend, I've been in the valleys, too. I know what it's like to have Satan using me for target practice. It hurts!

Do you realize how big a blessing we can be to others if we can get out of debt? It's God's desire to bless us to be a blessing, but we can't do that if we don't have enough for ourselves.

Here's how I handled it: I prayed for my financial needs and also for more than enough to help others. I didn't only want to pray for myself because I wanted to reach out with the love of Jesus to bless others, too.

We don't have to wait until we have a lot of money to bless others. We can give a little bit here and there along the way because there's an important spiritual law to remember here: "If you are faithful in little things, you will be faithful in large ones. But if you are dishonest in little things, you won't be honest with greater responsibilities" (Luke 16:10 NLT). The devil has deceived a lot of Christians by telling them to wait until they have more money before they help others. This is a bad idea because God checks our faithfulness along the way before He gives us greater riches. Let's first be faithful in the little things.

We can arise every morning and declare victory over our enemy and over every situation. We already have the victory that overcomes the world—our faith.[83]

---

83. 1 John 5:4

"You will also declare a thing, and it will be established for you; so light will shine on your ways" (Job 22:28). God's favor will shine upon us and He will establish our declarations. Hallelujah!

Jesus will cause us to triumph in every situation because we are more than conquerors.[84] We will overcome the devil by the blood of the Lamb and the words of our testimony.[85]

When I was a little girl and would leave our house to go somewhere, my mama would say, "Now, don't forget who you belong to." In other words, she was telling me I needed to behave myself because my behavior would reflect back on her as a parent.

As believers, we also need to remember who we belong to. Our behavior needs to be a good witness to others. We need to walk in everything He has given us, all of His authority and power. How we act as His children will reveal our God to the people around us. "Heal the sick, raise the dead, and cleanse those who have leprosy. Drive out demons from the possessed. You received these gifts freely, so you should give them to others freely" (Matthew 10:8 The Voice).

If we are going to be all we can be for Him and to use the gifts He has given us to help others, we must use the authority and power He has given us. Anything less than this will reflect more on Him than on us. We want to honor Him, right?

Prayer

Father, reveal to my friend the power and authority she has in the name of Jesus and that it's more than enough to move every mountain and demon out of her life. In Jesus' name, Amen.

---

84. Romans 8:37
85. Revelation 12:11

Chapter 5
Snared by Your Words

I read a book not too long ago, *The Substance of Things*, by the late Charles Capps, in which he gave a great illustration of how a seed manifests after its own kind.[86] He wrote that if we take a magnifying glass and looked at a newspaper photo, we would learn the photo was made up of a series of dots. These dots are shaded different colors to produce a recognizable scene.

Let's say that it takes two thousand dots to make a certain sized newspaper photo. The same number of dots could either produce a happy scene of a small child holding a bunny or a tragic one of an auto wreck. It's the same number of dots, but they are rearranged to create different images. Are you hearing me? "Now faith is the substance of things hoped for, the evidence of things not seen" (Hebrews 11:1).

Now, let's think of the dots in the newspaper image as our words—or seeds—which make up the substance of the photo. Our words can produce a good image or a bad one. It's up to us.

Maybe we're praying for a financial miracle from God. We even went to church one evening and gave a large offering, believing God would give us an overflowing abundance according to Luke 6:38. We speak our confession of faith: "I gave and now it will be given to me pressed down, shaken together, and running over into my bosom. As I gave, it will be given back to me."

---

86. Charles Capps, *The Substance of Things* (Tulsa, OK: Harrison House, 1990).

But what happened the next day?

The refrigerator went on the blink, the washing machine wouldn't run, and the car didn't start. What did we do next? Did we speak negative words? Maybe something like, "Well that's what happens every time I try to do the right thing. I give like God teaches me to give, then everything I have starts falling apart."

If we start speaking negative words contrary to His Word, we are rearranging things, much like rearranging the dots in the newspaper photos. It will quickly go from a happy scene to a bad one in our lives. "Do not be deceived, God is not mocked; for whatever a man sows, that he will also reap" (Galatians 6:7).

We can't let whatever is happening in the natural realm cause us to take our eyes off of what His Word tells us. We have to stand by faith, knowing God honors His Word even above His name.[87]

Let's allow His Word to arrange our dots the way God wants them arranged, not the way our feelings and emotions think they should be arranged.

I saw a good example of this when my granddaughter McKenzie visited me several years ago. She was not quite three years old at the time. One morning, we took her to IHOP for breakfast.

The waitress gave McKenzie a dot-to-dot drawing and a small pencil to keep her entertained while she waited for her pancakes. The dots were numbered one, two, three, four, and so forth. If a child followed the numbers correctly, a simple image would appear.

I watched McKenzie pick up the little pencil with her small hand. She drew a line this way and that way and this way and that way until it was a mess. She didn't understand the dot-to-dot idea behind the drawing. She just did it her way, ignored the dots, and scribbled all over the place.

I looked at her drawing and thought, *Lord, we're just like that with our lives. We ignore the dots You have given us and do whatever we want. Then,*

---

87. Psalm 138:2

we wonder why we're sick or have no money. A child has an excuse, but what is ours? Shouldn't we be eating meat by now rather than still drinking milk?[88]

We need to properly connect the dots in His Word if we want to live victorious lives. We can't rearrange His Word or change it and still expect to receive His promises, right?

We can't speak against what God has said about our finances and expect to get a financial harvest. Are you hearing me? We cannot plant seeds of strife or anger and expect peace. That would be like a farmer planting corn in a field and then being upset because tomatoes didn't come up. Wouldn't that be some kind of crazy farmer?

> Then God said, "Let the earth bring forth grass, the herb that yields seed, and the fruit tree that yields fruit according to its kind, whose seed is in itself, on the earth"; and it was so. (Genesis 1:11)

Every farmer knows the type of seed he plants will eventually come up as a crop in his field. This is a natural law, but it is also a spiritual law because Jesus referred to His Word as a seed.[89] He said it would produce fruit if planted in good soil.[90]

But also, have you ever noticed it doesn't take much effort on our part to grow weeds? They're like evil curses, popping up everywhere in our yards. Dandelions, crabgrass, thistles, and whatever else!

The same is true with our hearts, if we are not careful. You see, the world around us is constantly blasting its negative messages at us. It's so easy to pick up what the TV or our neighbors are saying and agree with them by speaking their words forth. And then before we know it, we reap what we've said and it's not what we wanted.

What can we do?

88. Hebrews 5:13–14
89. Luke 8:11
90. Luke 8:15

Foot Stuck in the Mouth, Sometimes

I still remember the day the Lord impressed upon me how His children were losing battles because they did not know how to wield the sword of the Spirit, which is the Word of God.[91] He whispered to my heart about His soldiers needing to be trained to speak His Word. Thus, Speak The Word Ministries came into being that day.

> You have made him a little lower than the angels; You have crowned him with glory and honor, and set him over the works of Your hands. You have put all things in subjection under his feet." For in that He put all in subjection under him, He left nothing that is not put under him. But now we do not yet see all things put under him. (Hebrews 2:7–8)

We should read these two verses every day until we have a fuller revelation of what it truly means. We must understand that the word "all" means "all" without any loopholes in it. God says exactly what He means and we need to accept it as truth. As the revelation of our authority grows, we will see big differences in our lives. This will be one of the end results of renewing our minds.

No soldier would ever dream of going into battle without first receiving some training. He must know what to do and when to do it to survive in battle. There is no other way around this fact. The soldier's authority to fight the enemy comes directly from the Commander-in-Chief.

God's soldiers need to be trained, too. There are no shortcuts here. We receive our authority from the Lord of Hosts to fight our enemies, who are Satan, his demons, principalities, powers, rulers of darkness, and spiritual hosts of wickedness, but our weapons are not M16 rifles.[92] We are armed with the Sword of the Spirit, which is His Word.[93] We need to know how to use His Word effectively to fight for our families, our jobs,

---

91. Ephesians 6:17
92. Ephesians 6:12
93. Ephesians 6:17

our health, our finances, and even our lives. His Word is our only hope. Praise His holy name!

As we continue to learn how to agree with God's Word, we will become stronger and more confident in Him. Our mountains will move out of our way faster and our faith will rise to higher levels. We will know God better and trust Him more.

> [You said to me] "Who is this that darkens and obscures counsel [by words] without knowledge?" Therefore [I now see] I have [rashly] uttered that which I did not understand, things too wonderful for me, which I did not know. . . . I had heard of You [only] by the hearing of the ear, but now my [spiritual] eye sees You. (Job 42:3, 5 AMP)

Job knew God before his trials began and walked as blameless as possible before Him, but Job only knew Him with his natural senses.[94] Thus, when Job received a deeper revelation of God, he saw Him with the eyes of his heart.[95] Then, Job said, "Therefore I abhor myself, and repent in dust and ashes" (Job 42:6).

Before I was born again, I had heard about God, but I didn't have a relationship with Him. Satan had put blinders over my eyes, but even after my salvation, it took a while to get my feet on the ground to walk with Him.[96]

One of the first things I learned was about sticking my foot in my mouth and then wishing I could take the words back. It didn't take long to learn I couldn't erase my words once they were spoken. "The heart of the wise instructs his mouth [in wisdom] and adds persuasiveness to his lips" (Job 16:23 AMP).

We need to understand that our spoken words program our spirits and our hearts for success—or defeat. Our mouths speak forth life or death to us. We will either be helped or hurt by our words. "You are

---

94. Job 1:1
95. Job 42:5
96. 2 Corinthians 3:14

snared by the words of your mouth; you are taken by the words of your mouth" (Proverbs 6:2).

Our words can trap us. So, let's be careful how we speak. "Your own mouth condemns you, and not I; yes, your own lips testify against you" (Job 15:6 AMP).

If we choose negative words, agreeing with our circumstances rather than the Word of God, with whom are we agreeing? Satan and his lying demons. There is creative power in His Word to help us, but don't forget, there is evil power in our negative words to hurt us.

"Set a guard, O LORD, over my mouth; keep watch over the door of my lips" (Psalm 141:3). David said in another Psalm that he purposed in his heart not to let his mouth sin against God.[97] We need to follow David's example and make up our minds to watch every word coming out of our mouths. Every word has value in the spirit realm, either helping or hurting us.

"Yes, again and again they tempted God, and limited the Holy One of Israel" (Psalm 78:41). My friend, let's not follow Israel's example and limit God with our words. The people of Israel fell short of the Promised Land because of their words. We don't have to fall short. We can renew ourselves so that our words move His angels on our behalf.[98] Every promise in His Word can be ours. Hallelujah!

The Power of Agreeing With God's Word

When we're going through tough situations, we need to search His Word and find scriptures that help pave our path to victory.[99] If we will start agreeing with what God says about our situations, it won't be long before we will see some changes there. Mountains will come down. We'll experience healing in our bodies and peace in the midst of our storms.

But to do this, we must walk in agreement with His Word. "Can two walk together, unless they are agreed?" (Amos 3:3).

---

97. Psalm 17:3
98. Psalm 103:20
99. Psalm 119:105

I still remember when I first prayed for healing in my body and began to believe the Lord could heal me. It seemed like the more I confessed what His Word said about my sicknesses, the worse the symptoms became. You see, this is a trick of the devil to get you to think that you aren't healed or that God didn't hear you.

However, I was determined I had my healing in spite of the symptoms causing pain to my body. The more Satan attacked my body, the more I proclaimed His Word over it. I said, "By His stripes, I am healed."[100]

I was sick and tired of being sick and tired. Can you understand me? I swallowed over one hundred and fifty pills a month and still felt sick. It didn't really matter whether I took the pills or not. They weren't helping me at all.

Hey, I know—it's tough to walk in faith! It's hard to keep your faith up when your body hurts, when everyone tells you whatever you're doing is not working. I can still remember being in my bathroom, throwing up. Who do you think whispered in my ears? If you guessed Satan, you're right. He whispered, "It sure doesn't look like you're healed. You're still in pain. Don't you know that if you really were healed you wouldn't be in pain right now?"

Satan was trying to get me to agree with him, but I kept on saying, "God's Word works and is still working. I declare full recovery over my body. I also exercise the authority that Jesus gave me in Luke 10:19 when He said, 'Behold, I give authority *to JoAnne* to trample upon the serpents and the scorpions, and over all the power of the enemy.' Thank you, Jesus!"

My friend, put your name in there, like I did. Make the promises of the Word personal, because whatever you're going through is personal to you, right?

I proclaimed, "His Word states He's given authority to JoAnne to trample upon the scorpions. JoAnne has power to put the enemy under her feet."[101] And I would continue saying what the Word said. "By his stripes JoAnne is healed. The Lord sent His Word and removed all

100. 1 Peter 2:24
101. Luke 10:19

65

sickness from JoAnne.[102] JoAnne is not moved by what she feels. She is not be moved by what she sees and not be moved by what she hears. None of these things move JoAnne."[103] Hallelujah!

Satan has had thousands of years of experience in deceiving humans, but still, we need to remember an important point: he can only do what we allow him to do in our lives because Jesus has given us authority over him.[104] He has no authority unless we give it to him. We possess overcoming power in Jesus' name. This does not mean Satan is powerless, because he does have power, primarily in deceiving us.[105]

"And they overcame him by the blood of the Lamb and by the word of their testimony, and they did not love their lives to the death" (Revelation 12:11). Did you notice what the believers had to do to overcome Satan? They had to speak and utter their testimonies. They had to agree with His Word. They became conquerors when they opened their mouths. Praise the Lord!

"For I will give you a mouth and wisdom which all your adversaries will not be able to contradict or resist" (Luke 21:15). Once again, it's up to us to open our mouths and speak His Word. Hallelujah!

When I was going through my healing battle in 1994, I heard a message about a minister praying for a woman who was dying of stomach cancer. The sick woman was skin and bones and could not keep any food down without throwing it back up again. The minister had just finished teaching on speaking to your sicknesses.

After the minister prayed for the sick woman, she said to her, "Every time, you throw up, speak to your stomach. Tell it, 'Everything I eat stays down. I am strong. I am healthy. I shall live and not die, but I shall declare the works of the Lord.'"[106]

The next time, the minister saw the lady, she was totally healed and had gained most of her weight back. She looked great—very healthy.

---

102. Psalm 107:20
103. Acts 20:24
104. Luke 10:19
105. Revelation 20:3
106. Psalm 118:17

Let's be honest—it had to be tough for this lady to succeed against cancer. I know in my case, I would wake up in bed and sit up straight to turn over. I would break out in a cold sweat when I did this, because the pain was so excruciating. But I would just keep thanking God for my healing. I kept praising Him and praising Him and praising Him. That's exactly what we have to do if we ever want to receive our victories, because Satan will fight us at every turn.

"Little children (believers, dear ones), you are of God and you belong to Him and have [already] overcome them [the agents of the antichrist]; because He who is in you is greater than he (Satan) who is in the world [of sinful mankind]" (1 John 4:4 AMP). God says we belong to Him. We're His little children. That should be enough to make us shout, but He also states that we have already defeated our enemies because the Greater One lives in us. He is greater and mightier than the god of this world.[107] Praise God!

> This command I am giving you today is not too difficult for you to understand, and it is not beyond your reach. It is not kept in heaven, so distant that you must ask, "Who will go up to heaven and bring it down so we can hear it and obey?" It is not kept beyond the sea, so far away that you must ask, "Who will cross the sea to bring it to us so we can hear it and obey?" No, the message is very close at hand; it is on your lips and in your heart so that you can obey it. (Deuteronomy 30:11–14 NLT)

His Word needs to be so near us that it's in our mouths and our hearts.[108] We are blessed when we hear His Word, but we must also obey and practice it every day.

Let's never forget about the benefits of speaking the right words out of our mouth. We will be rewarded for speaking God's Word, but we will also have to give an account to the Lord for every idle, inoperative, careless word we speak. [109]

---

107. 2 Corinthians 4:4
108. Romans 10:6–8
109. Matthew 12:36

THE WEAPONS OF A WARRIOR

Mark 11:23 reminds us we will have what we say. So we can't blame God for our poor harvests. We're the ones sowing the seeds with our mouths. You see, what comes out of our mouth matters because our words can trap us. They can keep us sick or broke, living on barely-get-along-street.

> How long must I put up with this wicked community and its complaints about me? Yes, I have heard the complaints the Israelites are making against me. Now tell them this: "As surely as I live," declares the LORD, "I will do to you the very things I heard you say." (Numbers 14:27–28)

God heard every one of Israel's words and was determined to give them exactly what they had spoken. It's one of His spiritual laws. Israel's negative words ended up causing their downfall in the wilderness. Will God treat us any different than Israel? His Word states He is not partial.[110] Thus, He will treat us likewise.

A priest named Zacharias and his wife Elizabeth prayed a long time for a child. Both were very old when Zacharias was chosen to serve as the priest to burn incense before God.[111] While he stood at the altar, he had a surprising experience.

> Then an angel of the Lord appeared to him, standing on the right side of the altar of incense. And when Zacharias saw him, he was troubled, and fear fell upon him. But the angel said to him, "Do not be afraid, Zacharias, for your prayer is heard; and your wife Elizabeth will bear you a son, and you shall call his name John. (Luke 1:11–13)

The angel went on to explain the ministry their son John would have in the years ahead. This same John would later be called John the Baptist and would go before Jesus in the spirit and power of Elijah.[112] So, how did Zacharias handle this good news?

110. Romans 2:11
111. Luke 1:7–8
112. Luke 1:14–17

> And Zacharias said to the angel, "How shall I know this? For I am an old man, and my wife is well advanced in years." (Luke 1:18)

The first words out of Zacharias' mouth agreed with his natural state, not with God's Word through the angel. The angel quickly reacted to Zacharias' unbelief.

> And the angel answered and said to him, "I am Gabriel, who stands in the presence of God, and was sent to speak to you and bring you these glad tidings. But behold, you will be mute and not able to speak until the day these things take place, because you did not believe my words, which will be fulfilled in their own time." (Luke 1:18–19)

Zacharias did not agree with His Word so God silenced him by taking his voice away. God's action stopped Zacharias' unbelief from hindering His plans by removing the biggest problem: Zacharias' mouth.

What If We Mess Up?

We need to stop our mouths from being problems, by refusing to give in to temptation and speaking before we think. Yes, I know we sometimes get angry and frustrated and words fly out of our mouths. Then two seconds later, we wish we could take all of them back. Sadly, it's too late, but there is something we can do.

> No weapon formed against you shall prosper, and every tongue, which rises against you in judgment you shall condemn. This is the heritage of the servants of the Lord, and their righteousness is from Me," says the LORD. (Isaiah 54:17)

When I say something that I shouldn't have said or know my words don't line up with God's Word, I immediately repent and pray something like this: "Lord I didn't mean to say that. This is what I meant to say." I then pray the right words, the ones, which will agree with His Word.

I don't stop there because I don't want my negative words to prosper. I curse my wrong words and command every word to hit the ground and not bear any fruit in the name of Jesus.

I pray the exact same way if somebody else says something about me, either in a letter, in person, or on the phone. I won't say anything in front of the person but as soon as I leave the person's presence, I pray against the person's words.

Remember, we are not always going to get it right every time, but still, let's keep on speaking to our bodies and our circumstances. The more we speak, the better we will become at using God's Word.

Keep on Believing and Speaking

> Look also at ships: although they are so large and are driven by fierce winds, they are turned by a very small rudder wherever the pilot desires. Even so the tongue is a little member and boasts great things. See how great a forest a little fire kindles! (James 3:4–5)

Did you know that it can take a mile or more to turn a large ship around? The captain must hold on to the wheel and keep turning it until he completes his turn. If the captain lets go of the wheel, the ship could go back to where it started. Most of the time, the passengers don't even know the ship is turning, because they don't feel anything.

It's the same way with us. We pray and we pray and nothing seems to be happening in the natural. It looks the same. But we need to remember that all the action is happening in the supernatural realm. Angels are ascending and descending on our behalf.[113] His Word is about the seen and the unseen. So, don't let the devil deceive you just because you don't feel or see any change. Trust me on this: changes are taking place.

It's not important what or how we feel. It's only important what His Word says about our situation. You see, the devil loves to play on our emotions. It's one of his favorite tricks to deceive us.

---

113. Genesis 28:12

> Now when the tempter came to Him, he said, "If You are the Son of God, command that these stones become bread." But He answered and said, "It is written, 'Man shall not live by bread alone, but by every word that proceeds from the mouth of God.'" (Matthew 4:3–4)

Jesus was hungry, but He refused to lower Himself to agreeing with Satan. He answered by saying, "It is written." And that's what we need to do, too. We have the same power living inside us that raised Christ from the dead.[114] Think about that for a moment or two. We have resurrection power inside us! How awesome is that?

We are no longer common natural human beings; we are new creations. The old things have passed away; all things have become new.[115] We are supernatural beings who can speak His Word to mountains, knowing our Father will back up His Word, and the mountains will move out of our way.

In fact, He expects us to use His Word like a hammer.[116] We need to keep chipping away at our circumstances—day by day, minute by minute, even second by second. Whatever it takes to receive our breakthrough.

"The things which you learned and received and heard and saw in me, these do, and the God of peace will be with you" (Philippians 4:9). God and His Word are the same.[117] Nothing is impossible for God and the same is true for His Word.[118] The Word will never fail us. The Word will always bring about victory for us. Our great High Priest, Jesus, has already ascended and passed through the heavens, so let's hold fast to our confession of faith in Him.[119] Hallelujah!

Faith has nothing to do with what we see or feel.

"Now faith is the substance of things hoped for, the evidence (or proof) of things not seen" (Hebrews 11:1). Faith must be perceived as

114. Romans 8:11
115. 2 Corinthians 5:17
116. Jeremiah 23:29
117. John 1:1
118. Matthew 19:26
119. Hebrews 4:14

real fact based on His Word, not on what our senses see or feel. Praise God! Let's keep on speaking His Word.

"And since we have the same spirit of faith, according to what is written, 'I believed and therefore I spoke,' we also believe and therefore speak" (2 Corinthians 4:13). We also must believe and then speak.

I am convinced through my study of God's Word and from personal experiences that God's Word takes on creative capabilities when spoken directly to our pain or our diseases or other mountains in our lives. This begins to happen the moment the words leave our mouths. His Word is Spirit and life.[120]

Prayer

Father, I ask that You help my friend to control his tongue from speaking negative words. I ask that You anoint his lips and put Your Words in his mouth, words of praise and thanksgiving, but when he falls short, help him to be quick to repent. Then help him to continue speaking Your Word. In Jesus' name, Amen.

120. John 6:63

Chapter 6
Hung by Your Tongue

I went through a trial a few years ago over the silliest thing: my windshield. The incident began when we were traveling on the interstate to a prayer meeting on a Saturday morning. A large rock hit my windshield. It sounded like a gunshot and made a sizable crack in the windshield.

A few days later, the crack spread across the whole windshield.

I didn't give it much thought at the time. My car had suffered hail damage the year before, and I figured I'd take it back to the same place. Then I remembered to file a claim with my insurance company.

When I phoned in my claim, the company referred me to a windshield replacement company in our area. The replacement company ordered the unit for my car and sent a serviceman out to install it a few days later.

The serviceman had removed most of the old windshield when he noticed something. "This replacement windshield is the wrong one; it doesn't have a sensor in it," he said. "I don't know why they didn't check it before they sent it out with me. But that's alright, I'll order another one for you. No problem."

He put everything back on my car and drove it into the garage. He packed up his tools, the wrong windshield, and left.

Ten days later, a different serviceman arrived at our house with another windshield. "Before I begin, let me check the replacement windshield first," he said.

He unwrapped it and checked it over. "I'm sorry, but this windshield is damaged," he said. "It has a big crack in it. But don't worry, we'll get you another one."

Another ten days later, I received a phone call. "Ms. Ramsay, your windshield is in, but it is also damaged in the same place as the other one."

By this time, I was really being tested. *Hello, Pastor Jo! You're being tested! Jo, are you listening?*

I immediately phoned my insurance company, and they called the replacement company. Everyone assured me they would get the windshield in right away and fix the problem.

I received a phone call on the following Thursday. "Ms. Ramsay, we've received your windshield. We'd like to send a serviceman out between 9 a.m. and noon tomorrow. Is that OK with you?"

"Oh, that sounds great," I said.

A few minutes after noon the next day, no one had shown up with my windshield. I phoned the replacement company. "I thought a serviceman was going to come to my house and replace my windshield this morning."

"Are you sure your appointment was for this morning?" asked the secretary.

"Yes, I'm sure. The serviceman was supposed to arrive between 9 and 12 this morning. I've been waiting!"

"Well," she said, "they haven't even picked up the windshield yet."

I quickly phoned my insurance company. "I've been with this insurance company a long time and I've never experienced anything like this in all of my life," I said to the person on the phone. They phoned the replacement place, and told me they were adding me to the end of the work list for a serviceman working in the area.

I thought, *Why would they put me at the end of the list when I've been waiting a month and a half? They should put me first!*

I was being tested! The devil knew how to push my buttons, and he was pushing all of them at once. It was ridiculous that I didn't recognize the devil's attack, but I didn't. Sometimes, we don't notice the enemy's handiwork until it's too late.

I eventually prayed, "Lord, I wasn't really ugly with all those people, but I sure wasn't nice to them. I was short and snappy. Forgive me."

We get tested from time to time, but we still need to treat people as we would want to be treated.[121] We must watch our tongues.

The serviceman finally showed up with my replacement windshield. "I've never put in this type of windshield before. So I've phoned two men from corporate headquarters. They're coming out to help me," he said.

The others arrived a little later and replaced the windshield in my car.

"I'm sorry. I didn't realize what you have been going through over the last six weeks. I had three windshields to fix today and you were tagged on to the end of my list," the serviceman said after finishing the job.

It turned out the serviceman was a Christian.

Thank God, by then I recognized I was under attack, so I wasn't such a bad witness with my tongue. We ended up talking about the Lord and I gave him a couple of my teaching CDs.

I certainly could have handled this incident better. Maybe if I had opened my spiritual eyes sooner, the test may have been shortened.

When we're in a trial, we need to pray immediately, "Lord help me to learn what I need to learn as fast as possible in this trial, so I can quickly get out of it."

If we don't learn what God wants to teach us in a trial, we will go through it again. (And for slow learners, maybe again and again!)

> To you who are ready for the truth, I say this: Love your
> enemies. Let them bring out the best in you, not the
> worst. When someone gives you a hard time, respond
> with the energies of prayer for that person. If someone
> slaps you in the face, stand there and take it. If someone
> grabs your shirt, giftwrap your best coat and make a

---

121. Matthew 7:12

present of it. If someone takes unfair advantage of you, use the occasion to practice the servant life. No more tit-for-tat stuff. Live generously. (Luke 6:27–30 MSG)

It's important for us to use every occasion to practice the servant life and to keep our tongues in check.

New Creations

When we become born again, our spirits are recreated. We are new creations and receive the nature and life of our Father.[122] Our language is almost immediately cleaned up. No more four-letter words. Yet our minds, which have held our spirits captive since birth, haven't changed one bit. They're the same. It's a little like taking a shower and then putting our dirty clothes back on again.

God loves us, but He wants us to renew our minds.[123] This is the only way we can have the things He has waiting for us in His kingdom.

In his book, *New Creation Reality*, E. W. Kenyon wrote, "Great enthusiasm and joy comes at the new birth for us, but unless that is cared for and fed by the mind being renewed through the feeding of the Word and then practicing it, that joy will soon die."[124]

Most of us remember the moment we accepted Jesus as our Lord and Savior. We remember the excitement and enthusiasm and how happy we were at the time. If you're like me and spend time in His word, seeking and talking to Him every day, your joy and enthusiasm will have grown since your salvation.

But sadly, many believers end up being so busy with their lives that they don't spend much time with the Lord after a while. They're still born again, but their joy and enthusiasm is gone. We need to come back to the place where we're excited to be alive because of Him.

---

122. 2 Corinthians 5:17
123. Romans 12:2
124. E. W. Kenyon, *New Creation Realities* (Lynnwood, WA: Kenyon's Gospel Publishing Society, 2000).

How do we lose our joy and enthusiasm for the Lord? "You are snared by the words of your mouth; you are taken by the words of your mouth" (Proverbs 6:2). Most of us realize our mouths can cause big problems for us, but it reminds me of my mom trying to tell me something when I was a young child. My standard answer was usually, "I know that, Mom."

"Well knowing it, Jo, and doing it are two different things," she would reply to my I-know-that response.

And this is true. Which means if you know this and you are not doing it, then you are probably in captivity right now. That's what it means.

Church Captivity

You know, the devil is holding much of the church in captivity today. The church has been bought and paid for by the precious blood of Jesus.[125] His Word states that God paid a high price for us, so we shouldn't be enslaved by the world.[126] Yet, sadly, we're becoming more and more enslaved every day, even though He gave His life for our freedom.[127]

Worse yet, the church is doing it to itself. We should be walking in total freedom because He gave us His power and authority to live here on earth.[128] Yet, how is this working out for us? His children are not much better off than most unbelievers. What do I mean by this? His children are just as sick and just as poor as our unbelieving neighbors. It should not be this way at all.

If we were the President's daughters or sons, we wouldn't be living in scarcity and want; we'd have everything we needed to succeed in our lives. Yet our Father is the King who owns it all and is willing to give it all to us.[129]

The only way we can break free from our captivity is to learn how to control our mouths. But to do this, we first have to learn how to control our thoughts.

---

125. Acts 20:28
126. 1 Corinthians 7:23
127. Galatians 5:1
128. Matthew 28:18
129. Psalm 24:1

So here's what I want you to do, God helping you: Take your everyday, ordinary life—your sleeping, eating, going-to-work, and walking-around life—and place it before God as an offering. Embracing what God does for you is the best thing you can do for Him. Don't become so well-adjusted to your culture that you fit into it without even thinking. Instead, fix your attention on God. You'll be changed from the inside out. Readily recognize what He wants from you, and quickly respond to it. Unlike the culture around you, always dragging you down to its level of immaturity, God brings the best out of you, develops well-formed maturity in you. (Romans 12:1–2 MSG)

The only way to control our thoughts is to renew our minds with His Word. It's our only answer.

Do you know why many people read the Bible? They think it makes God happy. I never do it for that reason. My desire is to know Him better and know what He has said. His Words are important to me and should be to you, too. How else will we be able to hold onto our peace and joy in our tough situations? We can rely on His Word to comfort and provide answers for us.

There is no other alternative. If we want prosperity, health for our bodies, and an overall prosperous life, we must renew our minds with the Word of God.

We also need to put the devil on notice that he can no longer trespass on our lives. We must begin to take back what he has stolen from us. "Yet when the thief is found, he must restore sevenfold; he may have to give up all the substance of his house" (Proverbs 6:31).

I can't repeat this scripture enough because it's a part of our heritage as a believer. I am a living witness to the truth of this verse. The devil has paid me back more than a hundred times over and above what he had stolen from me. How did I do this? I spoke His Word just like Jesus did when He said, "It is written."[130]

Wherever we are in our lives today, whether it's our work, our relationship with God, our health, our finances, or our family relationships, all of these are directly related to our mouths.

If things are going wrong for you, you need to have a little talk with yourself. You need to ask, "What have I been saying?" You see, we are going to reap exactly what we say, nothing more. Our words are seeds. So, if we don't like our harvest, we need to change our words.

Did you know that spirits follow our words?

God hears our words, but so does Satan. If for example, we continually talk about our lack of finances, the devil has the right to continue stealing finances from us. As long as we keep talking failure, we will continue to fail. Satan has a right to ride our negative words all the way to our total poverty. The same holds true for our health. We cannot continue speaking words of death and then expect to be healthy. It just doesn't work that way.

The late Bible teacher Charles Capps found an article in the August 1991 edition of *Reader's Digest* entitled "Patient Knows Best." The article was based on a simple question asked of twenty-eight thousand people: *Is your health excellent, good, fair, or poor?*

A follow-up study conducted four years later determined that how people answered the question was an accurate predictor of whether they lived or died during the four-year time period. Those who rated their health as poor were four or five times as likely to have died than those who rated their health as excellent.

Five other studies done by a sociologist at Rutgers and a doctor at Yale totaling twenty-three thousand people reached similar conclusions.

The research showed that people who have an image of themselves being in poor health repeatedly talked about their poor health. Their poor health image seldom had any basis in fact with their actual health at all. Most were in good health, yet their words were always negative.

---

130. Matthew 4:4

THE WEAPONS OF A WARRIOR

These studies confirm His Word: "Death and life are in the power of the tongue, and those who love it will eat its fruit" (Proverbs 18:21). This scripture used to be my license plate, but when I moved to Virginia, someone else already had it. That's OK! God gave me a new ministry, and now my license plate is Matthew 8:8. People ask me all the time what my license plate means, so it's a great opportunity to tell them about speaking His Word.

Satan may follow and ride on our negative words, but guess what?

> Bless the Lord, you His angels, who excel in strength, who
> do His word, heeding the voice of His word. (Psalm 103:20)

> Then the LORD said to me, "You have seen well, for I am
> watching over My word to perform it." (Jeremiah 1:12 NASB)

If we speak His Word, the Spirit of God and His angels will follow our words. Hallelujah!

You know, our heavenly Father wants us to live healthy and prosperous lives, but we must quit being hung by our tongues. It will take some effort on our part, but it will be worth it. "Those who control their tongue will have a long life; opening your mouth can ruin everything" (Proverbs 13:3 NLT).

The Lord has spent years working with me about my words and I still haven't arrived. He teaches me something new every day. The world programmed us since birth to think and speak a certain way, so it takes a while to change us, but we have a patient Father. Praise His name!

One thing I learned from my years of being involved in a prison ministry: prisoners have a lot of time on their hands. Most either spend their time sitting around or working out with weights. Those who worked out built up their muscles and were in great shape.

As I stood and watched some prisoners exercising in the prison yard, the Lord impressed upon me that this was the same way to build our faith in His Word. Yes, we need to spend time with the Lord and in His Word, but then we must exercise our faith in everything we do. We have to make up our minds to follow through on this. It's up to us!

The Lord Will Fight Our Battles

A while ago, someone snuck into my yard and destroyed some of my plants. The person did this several times over a short time period. I think I know who did it, but it doesn't matter because I won't do anything to the person.

It's not my battle because I sought the Lord on the problem. He instructed me to let Him handle it. I first prayed and then took my weapon, which is the Word of God, outside with me. "The Lord will cause the enemies who rise up against you to be defeated before you; they will come out against you one way, but flee before you seven ways" (Deuteronomy 28:7 AMP).

I prayed the above verse over my back yard and its plants.

The verse following the above one says we will be blessed in the land because we obey His commands and walk in His ways. When we follow His ways, the Lord will fight for us. Our enemies are His enemies. Praise the Lord! "The Lord himself will fight for you. Just stay calm" (Exodus 14:14 NLT). Another translation states that we must be quiet. So, if we want the Lord to fight for us, we must stay calm and quiet.

In simple words, if we give our situations to the Lord, we can't call our friends and neighbors to ask their opinion on what we should do. We have to do it God's way and wait for Him to take care of it.

This is called faith.

It works the same way when we need a healing or have debts weighing us down. We search His Word and find scriptures to use when we wield the sword of the Spirit to fight our battles.[131] We just keep speaking until we can touch the answer.

The Lord whispered to my heart in 2005 to start a ministry place. I called it A Place of Grace. A partner was supposed to help me in building and running it.

At the time, I was a prison chaplain and had been working in the jail and prison system for about eleven years. We worked with men and

131. Ephesians 6:17

women at the jail, but only men at the prison because it was an all male penitentiary.

A grant helped us kick off the project. Family and friends then volunteered to do the electrical work, painting, and repairs. We got it all done, but I noticed something. My partner refused to sign anything. I signed for everything.

After applying for a $200,000 grant, I decided to check our books. My search revealed that my partner had spent money to start her own ministry, a website, and other things for herself. All of the money was supposed to be used only for our ministry together.

I immediately closed everything down, even though the ministry had signed multi-year contracts. There was nothing else I could do.

My heart was broken because I knew the Lord had given this to me. Yet, the devil is still here on earth and works through people. But even so, we have to keep persevering and doing the right thing. We have to be obedient on good days and on our worst ones.

I prayed for the girl and would break down crying every time. My husband had passed away a short time before this, but her betrayal felt more devastating to me than my husband's death. I couldn't understand it, but the Lord helped me through it.

I made the payments on the contracts even though I was a widow on a fixed income. (But at the same time, let me tell you that I have never thought of myself as a person on a fixed income. God is my source; He owns everything. We have to have this mindset if we want to prosper in God's kingdom.) The Lord eventually brought me through this trial and paid off my debts. Hallelujah!

No matter what happens in our lives, we have to be faithful in doing the right things. "Repay no one evil for evil. Have regard for good things in the sight of all men" (Romans 12:17). Most people seek revenge from the people who hurt them. That is never God's way. If we persist on going down the revenge path, we will lose our battles. The only way to end up on the winning side is to do it God's way, by walking in humility, love, and obedience.

"For whatever is born of God overcomes the world. And this is the victory that has overcome the world—our faith" (1 John 5:4). My friend, if we have been born again, we are born of God. This fact along with our faith will make us overcomers in every circumstance we face. Let's walk in boldness, speaking His Word at our mountains and knowing our Father honors His Word.

Prayer

Father, place a guard over my friend's mouth and a watch at the door of her lips. Take control of what she says. In Jesus' name, Amen.

Chapter 7
The Power of
Right Thinking

In 2005, while I was ministering at the Duplin Correctional Center, an all-male prison in Kenansville, North Carolina, the Lord began whispering to my heart that He wanted me to become a chaplain. A few thoughts about being a chaplain had dropped into my mind before this, but I had not followed up on them.

What's odd is that I didn't even realize God was the one putting the thoughts in my mind. I thought it was just me, building sandcastles in the sky. It was a year before I took the first step to do anything about it.

You see, my old mindset couldn't imagine myself in that position even though God saw me doing it. It was His plan for my life. Looking back, it was sort of like what happened to Gideon when the angel visited him and said, "The Lord is with you, Gideon, you mighty man of valor."[132]

Gideon saw himself as a member of the weakest clan of the tribe of Manasseh and the lowest member in his father's house.[133] The angel's words seemed foolish to his ears, but God saw him as a man of fearless courage and the one to lead Israel against its enemies. Gideon eventually had to step out in faith and believe God's vision for his life.[134]

---

132. Judges 6:12
133. Judges 6:15
134. Judges 6:34

Whenever I thought about the position of chaplain at the time, all I could think about were the obstacles and barriers, and why it couldn't happen. North Carolina required a college degree and training to become a chaplain; these were not a part of my resume. How could I possibly get past those requirements?

Who is the one who always shows up to discourage us when God gives us an idea for our lives?[135] The devil, right? He constantly kept me looking at the obstacles and reasons why I couldn't succeed. I would never have become a chaplain with the mindset I had back then, which agreed with Satan's negative words.

But there was one thing I had not considered at the time: the God factor.

> And do not be conformed to this world [any longer with its superficial values and customs], but be transformed and progressively changed [as you mature spiritually] by the renewing of your mind [focusing on godly values and ethical attitudes], so that you may prove [for yourselves] what the will of God is, that which is good and acceptable and perfect [in His plan and purpose for you]. (Romans 12:2 AMP)

The Lord began revealing scriptures to me. He told me to confess and meditate on the verses to renew my mind and change my old way of thinking. As I agreed with His Word, my thinking changed. I realized God's vision for my life could not be fulfilled in my own power and wisdom, but it would take the power of the Holy Spirit, the Greater One who dwelled in me.[136] I began stepping out in faith and trusting God. Nothing is impossible for Him.[137]

"But God has chosen the foolish things of the world to put the shame the wise, and God has chosen the weak things of the world to put to shame the things which are mighty" (1 Corinthians 1:27). Why does

135. Revelation 12:10
136. 1 John 4:4
137. Matthew 19:26

God choose weak people like me to be used by Him? He knows we won't be able to boast about our abilities and strengths because apart from Him, we can do nothing.[138] He is the author and finisher of our faith.[139] Praise the Lord!

Was there more to the story about my becoming a chaplain?

Yes! I had to back up my new thinking by stepping out in faith and trusting Him to lead me step by step in my new position as chaplain. I needed to rely on His grace to equip me each day.[140] He's the Good Shepherd.[141] Hallelujah!

Maybe you have some dreams and thoughts you think might be from God. If so, pray and ask Him to reveal them to you in a clear way so you can move forward with them. It doesn't matter whether you have enough education or proper training, because God knows you can do it with His help. All you have to do is step out in faith and trust God.

Thinking in Our Hearts

"For as he thinks in his heart, so is he" (Proverbs 23:7). All of our spoken words come from our thoughts. So, let's take the time to check out our thoughts. Are they agreeing with His Word? Are our thoughts helping or hurting us? These are important questions to ask ourselves, especially if we need healing in our bodies or finances to cover our debts.

We must understand that every thought has the potential to be a creative power for good or evil in our lives.[142] You see, these same thoughts may end up coming out of our mouths as words or seeds at some time or another.[143]

Do you realize neurosurgeons have discovered that the speech centers in our brains rule over all of our nerves?[144] These same neurosurgeons

---

138. John 15:5
139. Hebrews 12:2
140. 2 Corinthians 12:9
141. John 10:11
142. Proverbs 18:21
143. Matthew 15:18
144. David Yonggi Cho, *Unleashing the Power of Faith* (Bridge-Logos, 2006).

state our speech centers have enough power over our bodies that by simply speaking, we can influence our bodies in a positive or a negative manner.[145] In other words, when we're speaking healing, we're influencing our bodies to move in one direction. But when we're speaking death and sickness, we're influencing them to go in the opposite way. "For we all stumble in many things. If anyone does not stumble in word, he is a perfect man, able also to bridle the whole body" (James 3:2).

The scientific study I'm quoting from states our bodies are wired for love and optimism, and not for failure and defeat. How do we express love and optimism? By our words. Where do our words come from? Out of our thought processes.

Research has shown that our DNA changes shape according to our thoughts.[146] For instance, if we are fearful or angry, our DNA tightens up. This fact should make it easier for us to understand how worrying can lead to sickness.

There's a bright side to this study, too. All of this can be reversed as soon as our thoughts are centered on love, joy, appreciation, and gratitude. Isn't this exactly what scripture states?

> Set your mind on things above, not on things on the earth. (Colossians 3:2)

> And now, dear brothers and sisters, one final thing. Fix your thoughts on what is true, and honorable, and right, and pure, and lovely, and admirable. Think about things that are excellent and worthy of praise. (Philippians 4:8)

Scientists estimate that each of us has around 50,000 thoughts per day.[147] On the negative side, this gives Satan 50,000 opportunities to attack our minds with his negative ideas. You see, the battlefield on which Satan fights us is in our minds. He understands that as we think in our minds and hearts that is who we are in our own eyes.

---

145. Ibid.
146. Ibid.
147. Ibid.

Yet, this should not be the case for God's children because Jesus gave us authority over Satan.[148] The devil should be the one trembling when our feet hit the floor each morning. We are supposed to have him under our feet.[149] Praise God!

Our emotions and feelings usually end up becoming intertwined with our thoughts, which produces words and behaviors that then produce more thoughts for us. All of this is how we react to events and circumstances happening in our lives. It's the cyclical pattern of how our brains work. We will either end up going in a positive direction or a negative one. Are you hearing me?

Toxic thoughts lead to stress, which affects our body's natural healing capacities. That makes sense, right?

Scientists have proven that over 75 percent of our visits to the doctor's office are the result of our thought life.[150] Fear and worry wear down our brains and our bodies. That's why we must renew our minds with God's way of thinking.

> The world is unprincipled. It's dog-eat-dog out there! The world doesn't fight fair. But we don't live or fight our battles that way—never have and never will. The tools of our trade aren't for marketing or manipulation, but they are for demolishing that entire massively corrupt culture. We use our powerful God-tools for smashing warped philosophies, tearing down barriers erected against the truth of God, fitting every loose thought and emotion and impulse into the structure of life shaped by Christ. Our tools are ready at hand for clearing the ground of every obstruction and building lives of obedience into maturity. (2 Corinthians 10:3–6 MSG)

148. Luke 10:19
149. 1 Corinthians 15:27
150. David Yonggi Cho.

Yes, we're human, but we do not wage war with manmade weapons. Our weapons are mighty in God to take our thoughts captive and pull down strongholds of fear and worry.[151] We do this by focusing on His Word.

Here's an interesting fact: fifty percent of first-year medical students end up suffering the same symptoms of the diseases they are studying about.[152] Why? This is what they are thinking about all of the time. As a man thinks in his heart and mind, so he will be.[153]

"My people are destroyed for lack of knowledge" (Hosea 4:6). I have included all of this information in this book to remind us how important it is to renew our minds. You know, if science agrees with His Word, we need to pay attention. There is no good reason to suffer from any lack of knowledge on our part when so much is readily available for us.

"How precious are your thoughts about me, O God. They cannot be numbered! I can't even count them; they outnumber the grains of sand! And when I wake up, you are still with me!" (Psalm 139:17–18 NLT). God encourages us to think about Him and His Word while at the same time He is always thinking about us. Isn't this awesome? Maybe we need to ask for divine downloads from Him so we can learn how to flow in His thoughts.

A Testimony

A doctor once told a Christian man that he was going to die from his sickness. There was no hope for the man. The man's dad had also died from the same disease years earlier.

The doctor's words were a death sentence for the man, which produced negative thoughts in his mind. The bad thoughts began sprouting and growing right after the doctor spoke them.

Of course, the man could have handled the doctor's words in a different manner. He could have been courteous, left the doctor's office, and said, "I rebuke these thoughts in the name of Jesus. These thoughts don't belong to me. That's not what God has said in His Word about

151. 2 Corinthians 10:4–5
152. David Yonggi Cho.
153. Proverbs 23:7

me. But this is in fact what God has said about me." Then, he could have quoted various scriptures to combat the bad report he received from the doctor.

But the man didn't do that. He accepted the doctor's negative words as truth in his mind. His body soon began to shut down. Fortunately, he had a friend who knew the power of thoughts and the power of God's Word. (Don't we all need one of these friends in our lives? In fact, wouldn't it be great to have four crazy friends like the four who lowered the paralytic down through the roof to where Jesus sat teaching a crowd?[154])

The friend began speaking God's Word over the man's body. The man paid attention and agreed with his friend's words. The man then began thinking good thoughts and speaking to his body: "These arteries were given to me by God so I bless them. These are God's arteries. I have His DNA and His blood flows through me."

He continued thinking and speaking like this all day long, even at work. This was probably the last thing the man wanted to do because his feelings most likely did not line up with his words of faith. Feelings are how most believers wreck their faith. We must set our feelings on the sidelines so we can think and speak God's Word to our mountains.

When the man returned to his doctor, he was totally healed, but there's more to the story.

The doctor showed the man an x-ray of the triple bypass he had received from an earlier surgery. The triple bypass was no longer needed because a natural bypass had grown up in its place.

Our God is an awesome Healer!

We don't need to get God to come into agreement with our words. This is not the solution to our problems, but instead, we must come into agreement with His Word. He is the Word and our answer for everything we need.[155]

---

154. Mark 2:4
155. John 1:1

> That if you confess with your mouth the Lord Jesus and believe in your heart that God has raised Him from the dead, you will be saved. (Romans 10:9)

Yes, we confess our faith with the words coming out of our mouths, but we also have to believe in our hearts and minds about what we're speaking.

> My son, give attention to my words; incline your ear to my sayings. Do not let them depart from your eyes; keep them in the midst of your heart; for they are life to those who find them, and health to all their flesh. Keep your heart with all diligence, for out of it spring the issues of life. Put away from you a deceitful mouth, and put perverse lips far from you. (Proverbs 4:20–24)

Let's always keep in mind that there is a heart and mouth connection for us. The two must be in agreement with each other.

Wrong Thinking Will Keep Us Out of Our Promised Lands

God brought Israel out of Egypt and promised the nation it would live in a land flowing with milk and honey.[156] There was only one small catch: the Israelites had to first go into the land of Canaan and possess what God had promised them. This required faith on Israel's part, but to walk in this level of faith, the Israelites had to let go of their old thinking. They couldn't succeed by holding onto their wilderness mentality.

"The Lord now said to Moses, 'Send out men to explore the land of Canaan, the land I am giving to the Israelites. Send one leader from each of the twelve ancestral tribes'" (Numbers 13:1–2 NLT). Moses did not choose twelve professional spies, but instead he chose twelve leaders who were the heads of each tribe.[157] The people of Israel considered each leader a mighty man of faith. These men were instructed to check out Canaan and see for themselves if God had spoken the truth about the Promised Land.

---

156. Exodus 3:17
157. Exodus 13:2–3

Moses gave the men these instructions as he sent them out to explore the land: "Go north through the Negev into the hill country. See what the land is like, and find out whether the people living there are strong or weak, few or many. See what kind of land they live in. Is it good or bad? Do their towns have walls, or are they unprotected like open camps? Is the soil fertile or poor? Are there many trees? Do your best to bring back samples of the crops you see." (It happened to be the season for harvesting the first ripe grapes.) (Numbers 13:17–20 NLT)

Moses wanted an idea about the people living in the land, whether they were strong or weak. He told the twelve leaders, "Be of good courage. Bring back some fruit as evidence to show us what the land is really like."

When they came to the valley of Eshcol, they cut down a branch with a single cluster of grapes so large that it took two of them to carry it on a pole between them! They also brought back samples of the pomegranates and figs. That place was called the valley of Eshcol (which means "cluster"), because of the cluster of grapes the Israelite men cut there.

After exploring the land for forty days, the men returned to Moses, Aaron, and the whole community of Israel at Kadesh in the wilderness of Paran. They reported to the whole community what they had seen and showed them the fruit they had taken from the land. This was their report to Moses: "We entered the land you sent us to explore, and it is indeed a bountiful country—a land flowing with milk and honey. Here is the kind of fruit it produces. (Numbers 13:23–27 NLT)

The gigantic cluster of grapes, the pomegranates, and the figs proved that God had told Israel the truth. Indeed, it was a land flowing with milk and honey.

Then comes the "but"—and there always seems to be a "but" when we walk by faith: "But the people living there are powerful, and their towns are large and fortified. We even saw giants there, the descendants of Anak!" (Numbers 13:28 NLT). The only things the ten leaders could see in the Promised Land were the giants.

Hey, I've been there at times! I know how the ten Israelites felt that day. When I have walked in fear, it has never mattered how much evidence God had already shown me because I always wanted more.

The Israelites felt the same way. They had plenty of evidence that God's promises were true by the fruit the men carried back to them. Yet, all they could think about were the obstacles.

"For we walk by faith, not by sight [living our lives in a manner consistent with our confident belief in God's promises]" (2 Corinthians 5:7 AMP). God had told them to follow His commandments and by doing so, they would be strong and full of courage.[158] He promised to always be with them.[159] What more did they need?

> But Caleb tried to quiet the people as they stood before Moses. "Let's go at once to take the land," he said. "We can certainly conquer it!"
>
> But the other men who had explored the land with him disagreed. "We can't go up against them! They are stronger than we are!" So they spread this bad report about the land among the Israelites: "The land we traveled through and explored will devour anyone who goes to live there. All the people we saw were huge. We even saw giants there, the descendants of Anak. Next to them we felt like grasshoppers, and that's what they thought, too!" (Numbers 13:30–33 NLT)

---

158. Deuteronomy 11:8
159. Deuteronomy 31:6

The Israelites' old way of thinking produced a wrong mindset in them, which ended up causing them to miss out on God's promises. They saw themselves as failures, and that's what they became.

Only two men—Joshua and Caleb—were able to let go of their slave mindset and trust God.[160] All of the others died in the desert.

We can miss out on our blessings just as the Israelites did if we don't let go of our old way of thinking. You see, our minds have been programmed since birth to think like the world thinks. We can change ourselves by renewing our minds in His Word, but the choice is ours alone. No one else can do it for us.

"I can do all things through Christ who strengthens me" (Philippians 4:13). If God asks us to renew our minds, we can do it. He never asks us to do anything we can't do with His help. And He will flood us with His power to strengthen us as we study His Word.

Think about this for a moment: what is usually the first thing a family does when a child is rescued out of a cult? The family normally hires an expert to "deprogram" the child. Why? The rescued child has been brainwashed to think like the cult's members. Therefore, the child's mind must be renewed.

This is sort of what the world has done to us since birth. We have been brainwashed to think the same way the world thinks. Our minds must be deprogrammed and renewed by His Word.

God wants us to see things the way He sees them.[161]

"Such is the confidence and steadfast reliance and absolute trust that we have through Christ toward God. Not that we are sufficiently qualified in ourselves to claim anything as coming from us, but our sufficiency and qualifications come from God" (2 Corinthians 3:4–5 AMP). This was one of the verses the Lord gave me to renew my mind. I memorized it and confessed it every day. It's refreshing to know our sufficiency and qualifications do not come from us, but from God. He is our source, the One we can always rely on to bring us through any situation.

---

160. Numbers 26:65
161. 1 Corinthians 2:16

We just have to keep this in mind: "And let us not grow weary while doing good, for in due season we shall reap if we do not lose heart" (Galatians 6:9).

Yes, it requires effort on our part to renew our minds, but if we don't give up, we will reap the blessings of God. For me, it has always been worth it to hang on and never give up. He has never disappointed me, and I'm sure you will discover the same thing for yourselves.

Prayer

Father, I thank You for sending Your Holy Spirit to help my friend renew his mind and to teach him all things so he can walk in Your promises and fulfill his destiny. Help him, Lord, to keep a guard on his mouth at all times. In Jesus' name, Amen.

Chapter 8

Take No Thought

O ver the years, I've learned that if God tells us to do something in scripture, we need to pay attention to it. But if He then repeats Himself by saying the same thing two or three times within a few verses, we need to underline it, circle it, write it down, meditate on it, and do whatever we can to understand what He's saying to us. This is God's way of shouting at us about the importance of these scriptures.

> No man can serve two masters: for either he will hate the one, and love the other; or else he will hold to the one, and despise the other. Ye cannot serve God and mammon. Therefore I say unto you, *Take no thought* for your life, what ye shall eat, or what ye shall drink; nor yet for your body, what ye shall put on. Is not the life more than meat, and the body than raiment? Behold the fowls of the air: for they sow not, neither do they reap, nor gather into barns; yet your heavenly Father feedeth them. Are ye not much better than they? Which of you by taking thought can add one cubit unto his stature? And why take ye thought for raiment? Consider the lilies of the field, how they grow; they toil not, neither do they spin: and yet I say unto you, That even Solomon in all his glory was not arrayed like one of these. Wherefore, if God so clothe the grass of the field, which today is, and tomorrow is cast into the oven, shall he not much more

clothe you, O ye of little faith? Therefore *take no thought*, saying, What shall we eat? or, What shall we drink? or, Wherewithal shall we be clothed? (For after all these things do the Gentiles seek:) for your heavenly Father knoweth that ye have need of all these things. But seek ye first the kingdom of God, and his righteousness; and all these things shall be added unto you. *Take therefore no thought* for the morrow: for the morrow shall take thought for the things of itself. Sufficient unto the day is the evil thereof. (Matthew 6:24–34 KJV)

Three times God tells us, "Take no thought." This means it is important for us to obey it.

Yet, as a matter of fact, how many of us by taking thought can change any of our situations? Can we solve our problems on our own? We seldom can and will most likely make our problems worse by dwelling on them in our minds. "People who don't know God and the way He works fuss over these things, but you know both God and how He works" (Matthew 6:32 MSG).

Do you realize Jesus was contrasting the Gentiles—or unbelievers—with people who know God—or believers—in this verse? He stated that unbelievers fussed and worried over these things, but believers should not fuss or worry about what they are going to drink or eat or what clothes they are going to wear. These are the basics of life, which we all need, and yet Jesus said, "Take no thought. Don't worry about them."

He told us to focus ourselves on seeking the kingdom of God and His righteousness and then the other things would be added to our lives.[162]

"Give your entire attention to what God is doing right now, and don't get worked up about what may or may not happen tomorrow. God will help you deal with whatever hard things come up when the time comes" (Matthew 6:34 MSG). Most of the things we fret and worry about never happen. It is just the enemy's way of stirring us up. Sadly, we often fall into his snares.

---

162. Matthew 6:33

Remember: the devil is always trying to mess with our minds. He wants us to be worried and upset over something all the time. It seems like this is Satan's fulltime job and let me tell you, he's good at it—if we let him trap us. He knows if he can get us to worry and be fearful, we are not going to get our answers from heaven. The Lord can't work with us when we're not trusting and resting in Him.

I know it is not always easy to do this, but we can do it with His help because the Greater One lives inside us.

Three Ounces

Last year I gained about 7 or 8 pounds. For many people, gaining seven or eight pounds is probably not a big deal, but it was to me. Certain things may bother some of us but not others. This just happens to bug me!

I was sick much of last year and took a medication that had a side effect of increasing my appetite. I kept eating and eating because I thought I was hungry. After eating, I would feel a little better, but five minutes later I was hungry again. It was a never-ending battle for me.

Finally, I was able to start working out again and watching what I ate. My goal was to lose the weight as fast as possible.

But a few weeks ago, a thought hit me as I went into my prayer closet to spend some time with the Lord. The thought came out of nowhere and nagged at me: *I need to weigh myself.*

Have you ever had a thought hit your mind and wonder where it came from? You weren't even thinking about it, but all of a sudden it landed in your mind and you had to deal with it.

That was how I felt that day. So what did I do? I ended up taking the thought. I owned it! I could have chosen not to accept the thought, but I took it as my own.

I still walked into my prayer closet without weighing myself, but as I began praying, the thought pestered me. Praise and worship music streamed through the speakers at a low level. My coffee and prayer book sat next to me, but that thought was stuck in my mind.

I thought, *I can't focus on the Lord. I might as well weigh myself and get this out of the way right now.* So I went and weighed myself.

How much weight had I gained? Not thirty pounds, not three pounds, but just three ounces. *Three ounces!*

The devil took those three ounces and used them to dominate my prayer time that morning. All I could think about were those three ounces. I couldn't even concentrate enough to pray.

Maybe you're saying to yourself, "How could a pastor allow herself to be so bothered about three ounces?" Well, I did, and that little fox spoiled my day.[163]

This is the important point to remember: it had nothing to do with my gaining three ounces. It could just as easily have been something else. You see, the main point is that I took the thought.

It's my belief that Satan customizes negative thoughts for each of us and drops them into our minds. This is one of the ways he attacks us.

Satan did a number on me on that day. It didn't matter that I gained three ounces because one ounce would have set me off. My hard work on the treadmill—fifty minutes per day—had accomplished nothing; I still gained weight. That's enough to make any woman upset!

All of sudden, I thought, *Jo, what are you doing?*

I began speaking aloud, "I don't have to take this thought. I can choose what I think." Then I began casting the thought down by confessing God's Word.

The minute I recognized I didn't have to take that thought as mine, I was set free from its power. "For the weapons of our warfare are not carnal but mighty in God for pulling down strongholds, casting down arguments and every high thing that exalts itself against the knowledge of God, bringing every thought into captivity to the obedience of Christ" (2 Corinthians 10:4–5).

163. Song of Solomon 2:15

When I began confessing and speaking God's Word to my thought, I brought the thought into captivity. It could no longer exalt itself against the true knowledge of God. The thought lost its power over me.

Our thoughts—good or bad—control us. There are consequences to the thoughts we choose to take and meditate on. They can be thoughts about our job, our marriage, our children, whatever. If the thoughts are good, they will agree with His Word and bless us. But if the thoughts are from the devil, they will always be contrary to His Word and may wreck God's plans for our lives.

Remember, we choose whether we accept a thought or not. We can always say, "Satan, I think I am going to pass on that thought. I'm not going to take that one." If he puts the thought in our minds again, we can pass on it once more and begin confessing what God says about it. That's how we bring the thought into captivity.

If we are caught off guard and react to a situation by thinking negatively, our mind will suffer. And if we continue thinking negatively, our whole body may suffer. Negative thinking spreads like a cancer, destroying everything in its path.

Research shows that our DNA can actually change shape according to our thoughts.[164] Fear, anger, and frustration cause our DNA to tighten up and become shorter. This action can switch off some of our DNA codes, which may reduce the quality of our expression and its power to voice a proper attitude against our emotions.[165]

There is another side to this because research has also shown the tightening of our DNA can be reversed by thinking thoughts of love, joy, appreciation, and gratitude. Isn't this what His Word states?

> Set your mind on things above, not on things on the earth. (Colossians 3:2)

> And now, dear brothers and sisters, one final thing. Fix your thoughts on what is true, and honorable, and right,

164. David Yonggi Cho.
165. Ibid.

101

and pure, and lovely, and admirable. Think about things
that are excellent and worthy of praise. (Philippians 4:8)

We have an average of fifty thousand thoughts per day. Some of these
thoughts are new ones, some are leftover from yesterday, and some may
be from long ago. These thoughts may be more dangerous than any virus
or germ could ever be for our health.[166]

My friend, whatever belief we hold in our subconscious mind may
become our reality someday. This is the power of our minds.

The *New England Journal of Medicine* published a study involving
two groups of people. Both groups of patients were suffering from
the same illness: a degenerate knee disorder. Group A's patients had
arthroscopic surgery on their knees to relieve the symptoms. Group
B—with permission of the patients' families—had a simulated surgery.
Group B patients thought they had a real surgery, but in fact, only three
small incisions were made on the kneecap.

What is really interesting is that both groups believed their surgeries
were a success. This is the amazing power of our thoughts and belief
systems. Researchers refer to the positive results of the simulated surgery
as the Placebo Effect. Most of the time we associate the Placebo Effect with
hypochondriacs who have been given sugar pills. The hypochondriacs
think it's a medication, but of course, it's not. Yet it still works on them
in a positive way.

Placebos help a high percentage of patients. It proves that many
patients have confidence in their doctors and the medications prescribed
for them. This confidence results in an improvement for the patients.

When you think about it, it's awesome how God has created our
minds and bodies. He fearfully and wonderfully made us in His image.[167]
I truly believe God designed our bodies to heal themselves, but we have
to get some things lined up to make it happen.

---

166. Mark 7:21
167. Psalm 139:14

We Are Not Victims of Our Biology

We must be careful what we are feeding our minds. Some things may be harmful for us to listen to or watch.[168] It could have a negative impact on our health. Thank God, we have the Holy Spirit living in us. He is our Helper who wants to guide us in everything we do. We just need to ask Him.

God created us to communicate with Him, not because He's lonely, but because He loves us. We are His chosen people selected to fellowship with Him.[169] Hallelujah!

We should wake up in the morning and constantly be in touch with God through the Holy Spirit all day long. We should talk to Him, ask His opinion, and seek His advice on everything. "But you have received the Holy Spirit, and He lives within you, so you don't need anyone to teach you what is true. For the Spirit teaches you everything you need to know, and what He teaches is true—it is not a lie. So just as He has taught you, remain in fellowship with Christ" (1 John 2:27 NLT).

God gave us a brain that is able to change from a negative thought to a positive one in a flash. In fact, our whole DNA system can be changed just as fast as our thoughts change. Isn't that awesome?

"For as he thinks in his heart, so is he" (Proverbs 23:7). We truly are what we think.

So, are we victims of our own biology? If our mom or dad died from a heart problem, will we suffer the same fate? If one of our parents suffered from depression, will we also have the same problem?

The good news is that we are new creations.[170] The old things have passed away and the new has overtaken us.[171] We are born into the family of God and His DNA is perfect. His blood has no bad hereditary traits in it. Praise the Lord!

---

168. Mark 4:24
169. 1 Peter 2:9
170. 2 Corinthians 5:17
171. Ibid.

We are first of all a spirit, or as it says in Genesis, a speaking spirit.[172] We also have a soul and live in a body.[173] Our Creator linked all three together when He formed us in our mothers' wombs.[174]

The only real weaknesses to our three-part creation are our mouths and minds. The words we speak and the thoughts we think can activate our old unredeemed natures. We can speak and think ourselves into heart problems and depression, but it's up to us.

You see, every word is at first a thought. We don't say or do anything without first thinking about it in our minds. Scientists estimate that more than 75 percent of all illnesses come from our thought life.[175] Shocking, right?

Once again, there is good news. We can renew our minds and learn how to rely on the Holy Spirit to help us. Then when our minds are under attack, we can cast down our imaginations and every high thing that exalts itself against the knowledge of God and bring every thought into captivity to the obedience of Christ.[176]

God wants us to fill our mind with His thoughts. David summed it up best when he said, "How precious are your thoughts about me, O God. They cannot be numbered!" (Psalm 139:17 NLT).

Where can we learn about His thoughts for us? In His Word.

Many people often say, "You know, we can't help what we think. It just happens." Is this a true statement? Are we just victims walking around and waiting for thoughts to fall into our minds?

We can make a difference in how we think. We can speak mind-changing words to ourselves.

For instance we can declare, "My mind is *my* mind. I can think about what *I* choose to think about. I can refuse to think about what I *don't want to* think about. I declare that my imagination is under the authority

---

172. Genesis 2:7
173. 1 Thessalonians 5:23
174. Psalm 139:13
175. David Yonggi Cho.
176. 2 Corinthians 10:4–5

of the Word of God. My thoughts favor others and myself, for Christ is in my thoughts. I take captive every imagination to the obedience of Christ. I recognize the power within me, believing I can have whatever I can think on or ask for. I choose to think on things above and not things of this earth. In Jesus' name, Amen." Hallelujah!

Stick a copy of this declaration on your refrigerator and read it at least once a day. If you need to read it more than once a day, do it.

> If you want to enjoy life and see many happy days, keep your tongue from speaking evil and your lips from telling lies. (1 Peter 3:10 NLT)

> You will keep in perfect peace all who trust in you, all whose thoughts are fixed on you! (Isaiah 26:3 NLT)

Our words and thoughts have a huge impact on our lives. We need to constantly remind ourselves of this fact. None of us have reached perfection with our thoughts and words as yet, but we can keep working at it. "Instead, let the Spirit renew your thoughts and attitudes. Put on your new nature, created to be like God—truly righteous and holy" (Ephesians 4:23–24 NLT).

Remember, nothing moves until we speak words. You see, our mountains know our unique voices.[177] Each mountain is not going anywhere until it hears our voice. It's kind of like some of the new security systems. These systems record a voice and store it. Then this becomes a person's password code to enter a place because no one else has the same vocal sound and voice patterns.

Someone can pray for our mountains to move, but our mountains will not move until we speak to it. It knows our voice, not the other person's voice. We are where we are today in part because of what we have been saying about ourselves. Words are like seeds.[178] So when we speak something out of our mouths, we give life to what we are saying. If we continue speaking it, it will eventually become a reality.

---

177. Mark 11:23
178. Luke 8:11

But remember, this works both ways. If we are confessing good things, the good things will end up being our reality. But if we constantly confess negative things, then that will be our reality.

Let's begin to call ourselves healthy. Let's call ourselves strong. Let's call ourselves prosperous. Let's send out faith declarations every day. Instead of saying, "We're never going to get out of debt," let's declare, "I will lend and not borrow."[179]

Everything I am today is by the grace of God and being obedient to say what he told me to speak. I had to bring my thoughts into captivity and speak declarations for my debts to be paid, for my body to be healed, and for my ministry to grow. I spoke those things every day back then and still do it today.

One of my declarations was, "Lord, I thank You that You are surrounding me with people who have big thoughts."

The Bible states that iron sharpens iron.[180] So we need to surround ourselves with people who think big and are filled with the Holy Spirit. We can feed off them and learn from them. We must change our small way of thinking.

Maybe we need to ride through some new neighborhoods and see how successful people live. Maybe we need to ride the elevator up to the top floor in office buildings, rather than going to the basement. We have to see ourselves in positions of success in order to break out of our same-old, same-old lives.

The Lord has often spoken to me over the years. Each time, I wrote down what He said in a book, beginning with a little blue one many years ago. Since then, I've filled several books, but my favorite one is still the little blue book. What I did was write down the date and everything I felt the Lord had said to me on that day.

He told me to write booklets and hold conferences. I have written eight or nine booklets and held conferences on an every-other-month basis for a long time. Now, my last goal is to publish a book.

179. Deuteronomy 28:12
180. Proverbs 27:17

The Lord never starts anyone at the top. I began washing off dirty tables in the forty-man cell in Duplin County, and preaching to drunks. Most of them smelled pretty bad, too. Many snored during my messages. Like most people in ministry, the Lord required me to be faithful with the little He gave me to do before He would give me more.[181] This doesn't mean I wasn't thinking about doing greater things for the Lord because I certainly had them in mind. I just knew it would not happen overnight.

How did I end up with the ministry I have today?

My one-word answer: obedience. I waited on the Lord, listened to what He said to me, and then followed His instructions. I obeyed even when it sounded crazy. You know, sometimes my natural mind couldn't wrap itself around God's thoughts right away, but He was always patient with me. Praise the Lord!

"'For I know the plans I have for you,' says the Lord. 'They are plans for good and not for disaster, to give you a future and a hope'" (Jeremiah 29:11 NLT). Our Father is always for us.[182] His plans for us are always good. We can take His thoughts and be blessed by speaking them, but we also must not give life to our negative thoughts by speaking them aloud.

Prayer

Father, help my friend say no to any negative thoughts and also to take any thoughts captive that do not line up with Your plans for her life. In Jesus' name, Amen.

181. Luke 19:17
182. Romans 8:31

Chapter 9

The Heart-Mouth Connection

E verything we receive from God comes by faith. It is the divine vehicle that delivers God's blessings to us. A simple definition of faith is a person believing that God's Word is true and then acting on it. "And it is impossible to please God without faith. Anyone who wants to come to Him must believe that God exists and that He rewards those who sincerely seek him" (Hebrews 11:6 NLT).

The Lord spoke to me once and gave me a great illustration of how to make faith work for us on good days and bad days. He said, "Jo, think of it as priming a pump."

I understood what the Lord was talking about because I grew up on a farm. Our home did not have running water or an indoor restroom. It was an old farmhouse with no frills, just a few bedrooms, kitchen, living room, and not much else. It looked nothing like our modern homes.

Sometimes, mom would send me out to the well to fetch a bucket water for the house. If the pump had not been used for a while I would have to prime it. A cup or so of water was needed to do this but if there was no water, we were in deep trouble. I would pour the water down through the top of the pump while I moved the handle up and down. The pump handle would dangle at first because there was no water pressure. I could pump it without much effort.

THE WEAPONS OF A WARRIOR

After a while, the handle would be harder to move up and down because the pressure would begin building up in the pump. I would feel the water moving up through the pump's system until it gushed out of the spout and into the bucket. It seemed like there was an endless flow of water.

This all happened because of priming the pump, but without priming it, nothing would have happened.

Sometimes we don't feel like praying or speaking words of faith to our mountains because circumstances have knocked us off our feet. Yet we have the Holy Spirit living inside of us. He is always ready to help us. All we need to do is open our mouths and start giving glory to God as best we can at that moment. A little praise and worship will start everything flowing. Then communication will begin happening between the Lord and us once again.

You see, we can't sit on a sofa and wait until we feel like doing something. Feelings will always lie to us. We need to prime the pump by opening our mouths and praising the Lord. Our faith will then kick in and we will be able to step out in boldness, trusting the Lord and His Word.

Keep this little story in mind for those occasions when your heart and mouth are having off days in the future. Our off days can be turned into opportunities to watch the Lord work in us.

A Prophecy

Before I mention the prophetic words I recently heard, I want to make a few things clear. Each of us is supposed to discern and judge prophecies for ourselves.[183] We are not supposed to be inactive listeners who just accept whatever prophetic words come out of someone's mouth.

"And let the peace (soul harmony which comes) from Christ rule (act as umpire continually) in your hearts [deciding and settling with finality all questions that arise in your minds" (Colossians 3:15 AMP). If we have any doubts about a prophecy, we need to allow the Holy Spirit to act like an umpire inside us. It is His duty to let us know whether the prophecy

---

183. 1 Corinthians 14:29

is from God or not. Usually, He does this by giving us peace in our spirits when the prophecy is from God.

Remember, if it's not sitting right in our spirits, then it's probably not from God.

I recently listened to some prophetic ministers speak about what the Lord was going to do, starting in 2017. One of the men prophesied that beginning in 2017, God's blessings were being released through our confessions. For your information, confession is another biblical term for "speaking" or "professing."

It struck me as interesting that the prophecy emphasized believers' confessions, which is what the Lord anointed and called me to teach to His Body years ago. I have taught countless teachings on the importance of believing with our hearts and speaking His Word with our mouths as confessions of our faith.

I don't study Hebrew so I don't know a lot about the language, but I did look up the seventeenth letter of the Hebrew alphabet. It is the word "Pey," which means mouth. Now, isn't it interesting that God has emphasized our confessions in the year 2017?

The prophetic minister continued to say that believers must learn how to confess the Word with their mouths to obtain victories in their lives. No longer can believers sit back, pray, and wait for God to do it. We must claim with our mouths God's promises for ourselves. Are you hearing me? "And since we have the same spirit of faith, according to what is written, 'I believed and therefore I spoke,' we also believe and therefore speak" (2 Corinthians 4:13).

The prophetic minister stepped on a few toes when he said believers must learn how to shut up and quit judging and criticizing other believers beginning in 2017.[184] Oh boy! My toes hurt a little because I've been upset with a few TV and radio teachers on how they seem to prostitute His Word. Yet, I've asked the Lord to help me stop being critical and judgmental of them. I'm doing better now by learning to let the Lord handle these problems and keeping quiet.

---

184. Romans 14:10

Hey, I don't want to be judgmental against believers and I'm sure you feel the same way. You see, the way we judge others is the same way we'll be judged ourselves.[185] We need to remember our words are like magnets, attracting good or evil toward us. Praise the Lord.

My friend, we must never forget the power of our words. Our words can either lift others up by encouraging them, or cut their hearts like knives with our criticisms. We can speak to our circumstances, bringing victory or defeat to us. It's that simple. So, let's continue to be careful about the words we speak.

Speaking Blessings

Let's say we are dissatisfied with our boss at our place of employment. What should we do? Should we talk to other employees about our unhappiness? Should we talk with everyone who will listen to our concerns about our boss, such as our spouses, neighbors, strangers on a bus, or whomever? What should we do?

Dissatisfaction with a boss or even the company where we're employed is a common complaint among people, but it also can be a huge snare for us. Our negative words can hinder us from receiving a raise or moving ahead in the company. God will not bless our careers if we curse others with our negative words. He will only bless us if we bless others.

Maybe we don't feel like blessing our boss and even feel he should be cursed. Yet this is not God's way of handling problems. We must follow His Word and not base anything on our feelings. God states we must be a blessing to others.[186] This is what we must do!

Who knows? Perhaps by being obedient and holding our tongues, we will end up being promoted to the boss's position.

How can we accomplish this? "But the word is very near you, in your mouth and in your heart, that you may do it. 'See, I have set before you today life and good, death and evil . . .'" (Deuteronomy 30:14–15). The decision is up to each of us. We can choose to speak blessings over our boss's life, over our boss's family, over our company, over our company's

185. Matthew 7:2
186. Matthew 5:44

112

business, over coworkers and their families, and over everyone connected to our company. This can easily be done on a daily basis.

God gave us a two-edged sword with His Word.[187] We can use our mouths to decree and declare His Word over our company and its employees.[188] By doing so, a light will shine on our paths.[189] Hallelujah!

The Lord gave me an important revelation at the very beginning of my ministry. It's one I try to follow every day. He told me that every word I speak has the ability to create and every word I speak is a seed, which will produce more of its own kind.[190]

If we are blessing others, we will produce more blessings. If we are cursing people, we will produce more curses. Whichever one we are doing, the same will return to us.[191]

It still amazes me how scientists have discovered His Word is true after all of these years. Scientists now know the speech center in the brain controls all of the other nerves. The Apostle James understood this almost two thousand years ago.

> Indeed, we all make many mistakes. For if we could control our tongues, we would be perfect and could also control ourselves in every other way. We can make a large horse go wherever we want by means of a small bit in its mouth. And a small rudder makes a huge ship turn wherever the pilot chooses to go, even though the winds are strong. In the same way, the tongue is a small thing that makes grand speeches. But a tiny spark can set a great forest on fire. (James 3:2–4 NLT)

James compared our tongues to a small bridle bit or a small rudder because our tongues control our bodies, like a bit does a horse and a rudder a ship. If we could control our tongues, we would be perfect. The

187. Hebrews 4:12
188. Job 22:28
189. Psalm 119:105
190. Genesis 1:11
191. Genesis 6:7

apostle eventually stated four verses later that no man can ever tame the tongue.[192] That is, no man can do it without the Holy Spirit's help. Only God Himself is mighty enough to control our tongues. Praise the Lord!

Yet, it's up to us to yield ourselves to God and His Word.

If we ask certain people, "How are you doing today?"

"Oh, I'm so weak and so tired," they may say.

Have you ever noticed how many people seem to be saying this all of the time? If only they understood the power of their words, maybe they would change their words. Their voice is connected to their brains and that's where the nerves receive the messages about being weak and tired. The nerves then respond by getting weaker and maybe even shutting down. This does not happen because of a one-time message, but many of these people speak these same words over and over again.

If we ask other people, "How is it going for you?" they may respond, "I'm so poor that I can't even pay attention! I'm barely making it!"

Their words may be intended as a joke, but if they continue poor-mouthing themselves, what are they doing? They are attracting poverty to their lives.

However, they could change their confessions. They could speak what His Word has to say about prosperity and say, "Father, I declare that I am a generous giver and do so without a grudging heart.[193] Therefore I confess that You will bless me and all my work so everything I put my hands to will prosper.[194] In Jesus' name, Amen."

Another example is a person saying, "I'm so old I can't do anything! I'm older than dirt and ready for the grave." This is a mindset and an attitude. It limits our health and our life possibilities. Don't put a voice to words like this.

Our thoughts intertwine with our emotions to produce words and behaviors, which in turn will stimulate more thinking. We choose how this cycle will end up by our words and our thoughts.

---

192. James 3:8
193. 2 Corinthians 9:7
194. Psalm 1:3

If you are a senior citizen, consider saying something like this: "I thank you, Lord, that wisdom comes with age.[195] With long life comes understanding. I thank you, Lord, that I will yield fruit in my old age and shall be very green and full of sap.[196] My God will reward me with a long life."[197]

That's what His Word states. We can confess it and then be able to do the work of a young person, no matter what age we are right now.

My grandfather was almost 99 years old when he passed away. Yet he went out in the yard to chop wood right up until he died. His age did not affect his ability to do things. Maybe some things were not as easy for him when he was older, but he didn't give into them. He was a farmer with a can-do attitude and had a mindset that said, "There's not a young man who can outwork me. I can still carry my own weight around here."

Let's think about Abraham and Sarah. Abraham was one hundred years old when he impregnated his wife Sarah.[198] Sarah was in her nineties. The couple must have been the picture of health for their time period.

Although I will pass on having a baby, I look in the mirror at myself every so often and declare, "Lord, I thank you that I am a daughter of Sarah. As she grew old gracefully, so will I. I am the seed of Abraham and Abraham's blessings are mine.[199] I thank you, Lord, that I have Your DNA."

We can all speak and believe something like this for our lives, right? Praise God!

We Need a Heart-Mouth Connection to Move Mountains

"For assuredly, I say to you, whoever says to this mountain, 'Be removed and be cast into the sea,' and does not doubt in his heart, but believes that those things he says will be done, he will have whatever he says" (Mark 11:23). This is a powerful verse about faith and confession, but did you notice the heart and mouth connection in it? Jesus clearly

---

195. Job 12:12
196. Psalm 92:14
197. Psalm 91:16
198. Genesis 21:5
199. Galatians 3:14

stated it takes a combination of the words we speak and the faith in our hearts to move our mountains. The two must be in agreement with one another. When the two are working in unity, we will see healing for our bodies, prosperity in our finances, and salvation for our families.

Yet we must also understand that Satan knows how to use the underlying principles of this verse against us. He will drop his thoughts into our minds and want us to use them, rather than speaking God's Word at our mountains.

Most people look at verses like Mark 11:23 and don't realize there is a reverse side to it. We see the blessings attached to the verse, but we don't see the negative side if we instead speak words agreeing with the devil. Much of God's Word has a pattern similar to the one in Deuteronomy 28, which states, "If you obey, then God will bless you. You will eat the good of the land, you'll be blessed coming in and going out, your family will be blessed, your enemies will be defeated, and so forth. But if you disobey, then these bad things will happen to you. You will be cursed here, there, and everywhere."[200]

If Satan can fill our minds and hearts with his lies, he may coax us to speak his lies out of our mouths. Then, his evil plans may come to pass in our lives. That's why he attacks our mind and emotions over and over again. He hopes to wear us down with his constant attacks.

"A good man out of the good treasure of his heart brings forth good; and an evil man out of the evil treasure of his heart brings forth evil. For out of the abundance of the heart his mouth speaks" (Luke 6:45). Jesus stated we eventually speak whatever is in our hearts. That is why it's so important for us to renew our mind with His Word. Then, when we are under attack by the devil, His Word will come out of our mouths. God's Word will transform us into mighty soldiers for Him.[201] Hallelujah!

Let's say you're in a crisis situation and your faith is at a low level. Every part of your flesh will want to scream words of doubt and unbelief, but just clamp your tongue down, and keep your mouth shut tight. Faith-filled words will turn our ships around, heading in the right direction,

---

200. Deuteronomy 28 summary paraphrase.
201. Luke 6:45

but words of doubt and unbelief will torpedo our ships, sinking them into the muck. At these moments, cry out to God and ask Him to help. He will do so because He loves you.

"And be continually renewed in the spirit of your mind [having a fresh, untarnished mental and spiritual attitude]" (Ephesians 4:23 AMP). God's Word supernaturally cleanses our minds and washes our emotions. It will even wash away the memories of our past experiences and the lies Satan has tried to sow in our minds.[202]

If we believe we are more than conquerors through Christ, we will walk from victory to victory.[203] You see, we are what we believe!

Not too long ago, a relative of mine died. I thank God he had accepted Christ as his Savior and would no longer suffer pain in his life. But when we were putting the eulogy together, it was hard to think of a lot of good things to say about him. He had lived his whole life for himself. That's pretty much the sum total of his life in that it was all about him.

As I sat in my chair at the funeral, I thought, *Oh, my! Do any of us want to end our lives in such a way that when others attend our funerals no one can think of anything good to say about us, except perhaps we enjoyed eating pepperoni pizzas and watching sports on television? What kind of witness is this to our loved ones and neighbors? What kind of rewards can we expect to receive in heaven?*

I constantly talk to the Lord and tell Him, "Lord, I want to make a difference in somebody's life today. I want to speak a word that will encourage someone. Lord, bring somebody across my path today so that I can be a blessing to him or her, whether in deed, or word, or whatever. Let me be Your mouthpiece and let me be Your hands today. Use me today, Lord."

These are my words, but anyone can use them!

I didn't become a Christian until late in life. So, I'm a late bloomer, but I've been running as fast as I can since my first day as a believer. For more than twenty years, I've been a minster of the gospel. It's my hope to

202. Ephesians 5:26
203. Romans 8:37

publish as many books, booklets, and videos as possible before the Lord takes me home. I hope to leave something behind that will continue to bless people for years after I leave this earth.

Shouldn't all of us have these same hopes for our lives? Shouldn't we want others to see Jesus in us? Well, I think so and hope you do, too.

Prayer

Father, I pray You open up the eyes of my friend so he will understand the important connection between our mouths and our hearts. Then I pray his mountains will move out of his way so he can walk in victory after victory. In Jesus' name, Amen.

Chapter 10

Taking Thought and Saying Winning Words

T he Holy Spirit taught me early in my Christian journey that my pronunciation of words was of secondary importance compared to the words I chose to speak. Our choices of words either bless us or get us in trouble. We can mispronounce words all over the place with little harm being done to us, but that's not true about the words we purposely choose to speak. Life and death reside in the power of our tongues.[204]

The Holy Spirit also warned me as a young Christian not to speak out of my emotions or hurts. He let me know it's better to keep quiet than to react to someone's hurtful remarks with cutting words of our own. Our feelings will always get us into trouble!

Do you realize the two words—*thought* and *thoughts*—appear in the King James Version of the Bible over one hundred and thirty times? This should be a clue to us about the importance the Lord puts on our thought life.

> And do not be conformed to this world [any longer with its superficial values and customs], but be transformed and progressively changed [as you mature spiritually] by the renewing of your mind [focusing on godly values and ethical

---

204. Proverbs 18:21

attitudes], so that you may prove [for yourselves] what the will of God is, that which is good and acceptable and perfect [in His plan and purpose for you]. (Romans 12:2 AMP)

Don't copy the behavior and customs of this world, but let God transform you into a new person by changing the way you think. Then you will learn to know God's will for you, which is good and pleasing and perfect. (Romans 12:2 NLT)

Many believers give their lives to the Lord, but do not bother to renew their minds. They are sadly ignorant of their heritage and what belongs to them in the kingdom of God.[205]

What would we do if we inherited a huge sum of money? Most of us would probably drop everything and try to figure out how to get at our money. If we had to, we would hire the best lawyers possible and fill out every legal form to get our hands on the money. Nothing would stop us.

And that's exactly what Jesus did for us when he died on the cross and rose again. He left us an inheritance, which is awaiting us.[206] It is ours! But we need to learn how to lay hold of it. The only way to do this is through studying and gaining knowledge of His Word.

"You know when I sit down or stand up. You know my thoughts even when I'm far away" (Psalm 139:2 NLT). God knows our thoughts no matter where we are located at the moment. He even knows what we will say before we open our mouths.

"You have tested my thoughts and examined my heart in the night. You have scrutinized me and found nothing wrong. I am determined not to sin in what I say" (Psalm 17:3 NLT). All of us need to be like David, determined not to sin with our mouths. It would save us numerous trials and problems if we would only learn to do this.

It's interesting to note that when we become born again as new creations in Christ, we clean up our words. We stop speaking four-letter

205. Romans 8:17
206. Ibid.

cuss words almost immediately. But because we don't renew our minds right away, we don't understand that the words "poor" and "sick" are also four-letter words. These two words go against what God has already provided for us.[207] It's not that God is not willing to give prosperity and health to us, because He is willing, but we just haven't learned how to receive them yet.

I don't claim to have all of the answers because I'm still learning. He's teaching me more every day, but it's a process of continually seeking Him and being changed by His Word. This process will continue until He returns or He takes us home. Hallelujah!

"Concerning the works of men, by the word of Your lips, I have kept away from the paths of the destroyer" (Psalm 17:4). King David told God that His Word kept him out of trouble and allowed him to avoid disasters. Because of this, David walked in boldness and had no fear.[208]

"And now, dear brothers and sisters, one final thing. Fix your thoughts on what is true, and honorable, and right, and pure, and lovely, and admirable. Think about things that are excellent and worthy of praise" (Philippians 4:8 NLT). Kenneth Hagin once said, "You can't control whether a bird lands on your head, but you have control over whether he stays there or not."

The same is true with our thoughts. We choose whether to meditate on a thought or dismiss it right away. It's up to us and no one else to make this decision.

"You will keep him in perfect peace, whose mind is stayed on You, because he trusts in You" (Isaiah 26:3 NLT). All of these scriptures reveal the importance of our thinking. We can't allow any thought to bounce around in our minds and disturb our peace. If we need to, we must take the thoughts captive that exalt themselves against the knowledge of God by using His Word against them.[209]

Each of us must start where we are at this moment to change ourselves in regards to our thinking. It's a learning process, but if we ask the Holy

---

207. Psalm 103:1–5
208. Psalm 49:5
209. 2 Corinthians 10:5

Spirit to help us, He will do that. The Holy Spirit will take us from where we are now to a perfect peace in Him.

Remember: perfect refers to being mature in Him. It does not mean we will always get everything right because this won't happen as long as we live in our fleshly bodies. But we can keep striving toward the goal of perfection, right?

When a thought becomes words and then slips out of my mouth because of my emotions or feelings in certain situations, I try to repent as quickly as possible. I say something like this: "Lord, I am sorry. I didn't mean to think that way and say those words. That is not what I meant to say. Please forgive me. This is what I meant to say—"

That's all we have to do.

If our negative thoughts or words are about a certain person, we can bless that person by speaking blessings over them. "Lord, I thank You that I know that person. She is such a great mother. I pray You bless her today in everything she does. Keep her in peace."

The next thing we will know, we won't remember what we were thinking about her. It will be gone from our minds. With God's help, we will get better every day and things will begin turning around in our lives.

Cigarette Testimony

This reminds me of my cigarette smoking habit, which plagued me for over thirty years. It was one of the first things God worked with me to change when I became a new Christian.

He pointed out that the urges and desires to smoke were based in darkness, but His Word was light.[210] God told me that every time I had an urge to smoke to speak His Word at it. And let me tell you, I had lots of urges and desires to smoke after doing it for over thirty years.

So, I learned and memorized lots of scriptures and spoke them at my urges.

As I continued to follow His instructions of speaking His Word, I had fewer and fewer urges. It took a few months, but then the urges were

---

210. Psalm 119:105

gone. His Word was like a laser light in destroying my smoking urges. Praise the Lord!

It takes practice to keep our words and mouths lined up with God's Word. The world had trained us in its ways for years, so it's not an easy overnight change for us. It takes a while to be renewed, but it is doable. We just need to focus ourselves on doing it, but the quicker we study His Word, the sooner we will see changes in our lives.

Of course, the devil is always nearby, trying to put his thoughts into our minds. "Be sober, be vigilant; because your adversary the devil walks about like a roaring lion, seeking whom he may devour" (1 Peter 5:8).

When I gave my life to Christ, I truly was a new creation.[211] Although I had been attending churches for years, I knew almost nothing about His Word. There are probably numerous people sitting in churches right now in the same boat I was in back then: ignorant of God's Word. Maybe they attended churches for the same reason I did, which was because I thought it was the right thing to do. It went along with my thinking about owning a home with a white picket fence, driving a station wagon, and taking my children to Sunday school. I guess that was my Great American Dream!

Almost immediately after my salvation, the Lord began teaching me His Word and about speaking to mountains. I had lots of them! And don't we all, right? If it's not healing, then it's our finances or our families. There is always some mountain which needs to be removed and cast into the sea.

"'Does not my word burn like fire?' says the LORD. 'Is it not like a mighty hammer that smashes a rock to pieces?'" (Jeremiah 23:29). Mountains are just puffed up rocks. They are not a problem for God and His Word to handle. I am living proof that His Word works.

Are you talking yourself into an early death? Are you talking yourself into poverty? Are you talking yourself into being fearful and depressed?

These are tough questions, but we must search ourselves and ask them.

---

211. 2 Corinthians 5:17

Everything I teach I have learned the hard way because the lessons came out of my own life. I spoke sickness over my body. I spoke poverty over myself, not realizing the impact my words were having on my life.

I took over one hundred and fifty pills each month. Yet, I was still sick and getting worse. I know what it is like to be so sick that every part of me hurt. And depression? I could have been the poster child for this terrible affliction. I didn't care if the house was clean or my clothes were clean or if I ate anything because I was miserable.

Then, the Lord showed me how to pray and speak to these mountains. Some of them were removed right away and others took months or even longer. But today, I no longer take any pills, I am not depressed, and my debts are gone.

What Do You Have to Lose?

OK, my friend, what do you have to lose? If it worked for me, it will work for you, too. God is not a respecter of persons.[212] I believe the best way to stay healthy is to study His Word and keep speaking it over our bodies.

Let me tell you this: I am not against going to a doctor. I try my best not to go to one, but if it becomes necessary, I go. Some issues can be healed instantly, some take a little longer, and some we need to go to doctors and have them check us out. We can always mix our faith with what the doctor prescribes for us.

Recently, I had an issue with my shoulder and went to a doctor. The doctor couldn't see anything wrong with my shoulder, but I told him, "It hurts. There's something wrong."

He prescribed a cream to handle the pain I felt in my shoulder.

When my husband David rubbed the cream on my shoulder, I prayed, "Lord, I thank You that I can mix this cream with my faith. In Jesus' name, I thank You I'm healed."

212. Acts 10:34

124

God doesn't really care if we take a cream or a pill as long as we trust Him to heal us. He's the Healer. Our healing will come from Him. Praise God!

The Greater One Lives in Us

"You are of God, little children, and have overcome them, because He who is in you is greater than he who is in the world" (1 John 4:4). We are God's temple and He lives in us. Whatever hardships we may be going through, we never have to go through it alone. He lives in us. Not only that, but He has already won the victory for us because we are more than conquerors before we even start.[213] How do you like that?

> But what does it say? "The word is near you, in your mouth and in your heart" (that is, the word of faith which we preach): that if you confess with your mouth the Lord Jesus and believe in your heart that God has raised Him from the dead, you will be saved. (Romans 10:8–9)

Our miracles always begin with His Word being imprinted on our hearts and then speaking them out of our mouths. I can still remember the Lord whispering to my heart, "Jo, you got born again by confessing with your mouth that Jesus is Lord and believing in your heart. That's the same way you get everything else: by believing it in your heart and speaking it out of your mouth."

It doesn't matter if we don't feel anything or see anything happening because our faith-filled words are working in the spirit realm. That's where the action is taking place on our behalf. We just have to stay patient, stand in faith, and trust Him.

One of my declarations: "Thank You, Lord, that Your Word is working on my mountain. It doesn't look any smaller right now, but I know it is because Your Word does not return to You void.[214] It is always doing exactly what You intend it to do. I thank You that I am

213. Romans 8:37
214. Isaiah 55:11

125

not moved by what I see in the natural because my mountain is gone in Jesus' name, Amen."

"The seed is the Word of God" (Luke 8:11). I can't repeat this truth often enough in this book. It's a revelation we all must have to walk in faith and receive our miracles.

Perhaps this revelation comes a little easier for me because my father was a sharecrop farmer in North Carolina. I often worked in the fields, helping my father with his work. He knew if he wanted to harvest a crop, he had to first plant seeds in the ground.

The seed we plant by faith is every action, every word, everything we do to make His Word come to pass in our lives. I realize that a lot of people have given seeds a bad name because of false prosperity teachings. Sadly, some have even prostituted God's Word for money.

I don't ever want to be guilty of selling God's Word. Everything the Lord has called me to do has been on a volunteer basis. Yet with so many things, like speaking in tongues and laying hands on the sick, there are those who have different opinions and try to give these truths bad names, too.[215] But it doesn't change the truth of God's Word, does it?

"Then Jesus said to them, 'If you can't understand the meaning of this parable, how will you understand all the other parables?'" (Mark 4:13). Mark tells the parable of the sower a little differently than Luke does, but it is still the same parable. Jesus' audience understood sowing seeds and reaping a harvest because farming was a big part of their lives. So when He referred to God's Word being a seed, they understood the whole process.

The very moment something happens to us, the words that come out of our spirits are the words that will activate our faith systems. These are the words that will either put us on top of our mountains or under them. Are you hearing me?

Our first words are crucial. We need to carefully choose them.

In 1996, I was living in Warsaw, North Carolina. That was the year a huge hurricane came through our area. Although we had only lived

---

215. Mark 16:17–18

there for a few months, my late husband was busy traveling all over the county, making sure everyone was as safe as possible. That was his job as the Duplin County Manager.

Because of this, he was not able to be home to help secure our property and belongings. That was up to me. My five-year-old granddaughter Laura was helping me. We carried a table and some chairs off the porch and were heading to the garage. As I stepped off the porch steps, my right foot dropped into a hole. I immediately fell down. My granddaughter rushed over to me. "Gigi, are you okay?" she asked. (All my grandchildren call me Gigi.) "Should we call Papa?"

"No, Sugar," I said. "Papa's busy, but we are going to be fine. You know, we are not alone. God and His Angels are with us. They're going to help us."

I prayed over my foot and began thanking God for healing it. The pain had not lessened one bit when I finished praying.

You see, this is where a lot of us get confused because the devil works on us and tells us we didn't receive our healing. But we can't listen to him just because the symptoms are still there. We must walk by faith and not by sight.[216]

I have had numerous faith victories but most of them haven't happened right away. I had to continue using His Word as a hammer against my mountains.[217] Hammer, hammer, hammer!

However, in this case, I had to keep moving. The hurricane was almost upon us. Work had to be finished before the storm arrived. I continued walking on my painful foot, but it was only by the grace of God I was able to move around. All the time, I kept thanking God for healing my foot.

I went back onto the same porch to get another chair to take to the garage. Wouldn't you know it? I stepped off the porch and stepped down into the same hole again! Same foot. Same hole. And again I prayed and rebuked the devil. I pleaded the blood of Jesus over my foot.

---

216. 2 Corinthians 5:7
217. Jeremiah 23:29

My foot hurt all afternoon and then it began to swell up. By nightfall, it was in bad shape. I still remember sitting on the sofa in our sunroom. I looked at my foot, which was propped up on pillows, and said, "Thank you, Jesus, for healing my foot. I am not moved by what I see, but what I believe from God's Word. And His Word states that by His stripes I am healed."[218]

It hurt and did not look healed at all.

Everyone gathered at our home to wait out the hurricane. We were going to move into the basement but the heavy rain caused it to be flooded. Thus, we slept wherever we could on the first floor, rather than going upstairs to the second floor. Nobody wanted to sleep upstairs during the storm. I slept on the sofa that night. My foot was still swelled up and ached, but somehow I fell asleep.

I awakened the next morning and forgot all about my foot. I walked into the kitchen and began preparing breakfast for everyone. Then, all of a sudden I realized my foot was no longer hurting. Hallelujah! Thank you, Jesus!

When was my foot healed? The following morning when the pain left and the swelling was gone? Or was it healed when I prayed? These are important questions to ask because we must understand the healing process according to scriptural principles.

Many people think that most healings occur instantaneously, but the Bible says they shall recover.[219] My healing took place the moment I prayed for it, but the full manifestation took a little longer.

This story could have ended much differently for me if I had not spoken God's Word over my foot. As a matter of fact, two others in my family have had similar falls. Both are still having problems with their feet. One of them has had five or six operations and cannot wear certain shoes. The other one is better, but still has problems.

Before this happened, I had been filling my spirit with faith words for quite a few months. But even so, I could have easily spoken death

218. 1 Peter 2:24
219. Mark 16:18

128

over my foot. The Lord tells us we have a choice in what we say in our calamities. We can speak life or death.[220]

"A word out of your mouth may seem of no account, but it can accomplish nearly anything—or destroy it!" (James 3:5 MSG). When a crisis hits us and we're under pressure, we will speak whatever fills our hearts. If our hearts are filled with doubt, we will speak doubt, but if our hearts are filled with His Word, we will speak God's Word. Our first words may end up determining our outcomes.

We need to prepare ourselves now.

Prayer

Father, reveal to my friend the importance of taking her thoughts captive and speaking winning words to her mountains. Let her see victory after victory as she seeks You. In Jesus' name, Amen.

---

220. Proverbs 18:21

Chapter 11
The Weapon of the Word

H ave you ever felt battered and bloodied by someone's words?

That was my condition not long ago when I received an email from a person. The words leaped off the email and cut my heart like a surgeon's scalpel. People don't realize how much damage they can do with their words. They don't understand the power behind their words. That's why His Word encourages us to be swift to hear and slow to speak.[221] King David said he would keep a bridle on his tongue so that he would not sin against the Lord.[222]

Every word I read in the email bruised and battered me even more. *O Lord, help me,* I thought. *Help me, Lord!*

The person who wrote the email was someone I really cared about. Doesn't it seem like the ones we love can hurt us the most? Their words seem to cut deeper. Others can hurt us, but it's nothing compared to a person who is close to our heart.

The person who did this allowed the devil and his demons to deceive her. Usually, Satan plants a small seed of a thought in a person's mind. As the person meditates on Satan's words, the thought begins to grow. The devil knows exactly what type of thought a person will buy into and believe. These are seeds of deception, not truths. The seed does not

221. James 1:19
222. Psalm 39:1

bloom in one day because it takes time to bring the seed to full maturity. Then, the person spews forth her stinging words on her victim.

A person who hears abusive words, or reads them in an email like I did, is hurt and wounded. We can't understand what happened. Confusion hits us. Then Satan plants thoughts in our minds which can fester into open sores of unforgiveness.

Just when we think we have a handle on everything, Satan speaks to our hearts, "Don't you remember when he did that? Or when she said that? You can't actually forgive them! How can you ever think about doing something like that?"

I've heard people say, "Pastor Jo, you don't know what they've done to me!"

"No, I don't," I say, "but what they did to you was not worse than what we did to Jesus. And He forgave all of us and said, 'Father, don't hold this against them.'"[223]

We can't receive anything from God without having a forgiving heart.[224] We're all human and we all struggle with forgiving people who have deeply hurt us. But we have no choice and need to be quick to repent.

My prayer of repentance goes something like this: "Lord, I'm sorry I had those thoughts. If there is any unforgiveness in my heart, forgive me. I repent of that sin right now. Father, I want to have a clean slate before You. I want my prayers to be answered without any hindrances."

We need to walk in God's love and forgive others even when we don't feel like it. My advice for people who have been hurt is to go into your prayer closet and cry about it, but also forgive them. I've stood there many times in my prayer closet with tears dripping from my eyes and praying, "Lord, I give it to You. I forgive them. Would You please forgive them, too?"

After I read the email, I couldn't even pray. Words escaped my mind.

223. Luke 23:34
224. Mark 11:25–26

Have you ever been hurt so bad that you couldn't even pray about it? Perhaps you even felt guilty about not being able to pray. Don't worry about it, because we have all been there at one time or another.

I couldn't pray for hours after reading the email. I sat there hurting and feeling sorry for myself. My mind tried to unscramble her words and figure out where it came from. *Why? Why?* This was exactly what Satan hoped my reaction would be to the email.

Then all of a sudden, the Holy Spirit whispered to my heart and revealed what I needed to do. He told me if I wanted to win the battle that I must quit fighting the devil on his battleground because I could never defeat him there. The devil's territory was the arena of bad thoughts and unforgiveness. I needed to fight the devil on holy ground by using God's Word.

I chose to believe the Holy Spirit and follow His instructions.

So, I removed my sword of the Spirit from its sheath and began wielding it.[225] I spoke with my mouth and began slashing through the garbage in my mind with His Word. "Lord, I forgive that person. I love her and I know she loves me. I'm thankful You told me to bring every thought into captivity that exalts itself against the true knowledge of God.[226] That's what I'm doing right now with my words. Lord, maybe in the natural I don't have the ability to forgive that person right now, but the love of God has been shed in my heart by the Holy Spirit.[227] And that love of God can forgive anything and anybody. I give You all the praise and glory, in Jesus' name, Amen."

We stand strong and firm, continuing to wield the sword of the Spirit until the battle is over. Satan has no choice but to flee from us, but don't put the sword of the Spirit on a shelf and forget about it. Keep it handy because there will always be more battles in the future.

"These things I have spoken to you, that in Me you may have peace. In the world you will have tribulation; but be of good cheer, I have

---

225. Ephesians 6:17
226. 2 Corinthians 10:5
227. Romans 5:5

overcome the world" (John 16:33). I would not have won the battle without using His Word as a weapon. Praise His holy name!

Satan's Biggest Weapon is Deception

One of Satan's most powerful weapons against us is deception.[228] Even though we have a far stronger weapon in His Word, he tricks us into looking away from God's Word toward religious and spiritual-sounding ideas. We end up praying prayers without power and worshipping Him without His presence. We settle for a tickle-your-ears religion.[229]

Let's say we're praying for our healing and say something like, "Well, I believe God is going to heal me."

No, this is wrong!

"Who Himself bore our sins in His own body on the tree, that we, having died to sins, might live for righteousness—by whose stripes you were healed" (1 Peter 2:24). His Word does not state He will heal you, but it plainly states He has already healed you. This is written in the past tense. It's an already a done deal for us!

"He spoke the word that healed you, that pulled you back from the brink of death" (Psalm 107:20 MSG). This is His Word. This is our weapon against any sickness we might be suffering. God wants us to remind Him of His Word. [230]

> Just as rain and snow descend from the skies and don't go back until they've watered the earth, doing their work of making things grow and blossom, producing seed for farmers and food for the hungry, so will the words that come out of My mouth not come back empty-handed. They'll do the work I sent them to do, they'll complete the assignment I gave them. (Isaiah 55:10–11 MSG)

How do God's Words return to Him? Do they bounce off the earth? No! It's up to us to pick up His Word, put Him in remembrance, and

228. 2 Thessalonians 2:10
229. 2 Timothy 4:3
230. Isaiah 43:26

PASTOR JOANNE RAMSAY

pray His Word back to Him. We have an active part to play in all of this. That's why He says for us to argue with Him and plead our case.[231]

If we want healing by using 1 Peter 2:24, we have to use our mouths and return the Word to God with our own words. We must say, "It is written that I am healed." Or if we're using Psalms 107:20 for our healing, then we say, "You sent Your Word and healed me."

"My son, give attention to my words; incline your ear to my sayings" (Proverbs 4:20). We have to say what His Word states and trust Him to bring it to pass. God means exactly what He says and honors His Word.[232]

The devil plays with our emotions, trying to keep us from being as powerful as God has created and anointed us to be, but we must remember the Spirit of God lives in us.[233] Not only that, Jesus gave us authority over Satan and demons.[234] We are heirs and fellow heirs with Christ Jesus.[235]

Worrying should be the furthest thing from our minds. So let's not allow the devil to deceive us. You see, Satan is not as tough as we sometimes think he is because he is a defeated foe.[236] "Be sober, be vigilant; because your adversary the devil walks about like a roaring lion, seeking whom he may devour" (1 Peter 5:8). Satan is like a roaring lion, but there is only one lion that really matters, and that's the Lion of Judah.[237] Hallelujah!

God has given us His Word. When we speak God's Word, hell shakes and demons flee. We need to climb out of bed in the morning and begin the day by declaring and decreeing His Word over our lives. "No weapon formed against me today shall prosper.[238] No weapon of infirmity, no weapon of doubt, no weapon of fear formed against me shall prosper. Everything I do and touch today will prosper because it is

---

231. Ibid.
232. Psalm 103:20
233. Romans 8:11
234. Luke 10:19
235. Romans 8:17
236. Colossians 2:15
237. Revelation 5:5
238. Isaiah 54:17

135

written that I am like a tree planted by the rivers of water. I shall bring forth good fruit."[239]

Satan and his demons have already experienced firsthand what God's Word can do. They know His power better than we do.

"Having disarmed principalities and powers, Jesus made a public spectacle of them, triumphing over them in it" (Colossians 2:15). Jesus reduced Satan's actual power over us to zero at the cross, but we must enforce the truth of this verse by speaking it. There is no way Satan can withstand the power of His Word when a believer speaks it in faith.

I like to think that His Word contains God's DNA in it. His Word is pure.[240] His Word is Spirit and life.[241] His Word is Jesus Himself.[242] In fact, let's check out a special verse.

> For the word of God is living and powerful, and sharper than any two-edged sword, piercing even to the division of soul and spirit, and of joints and marrow, and is a discerner of the thoughts and intents of the heart. (Hebrews 4:12)

The Greek word "distomos" is translated into the English word "two-edged." The adjective—two-edged—means both sides are sharpened. It figuratively penetrates at every contact point, coming in or going out.

Historians have described the two-edged sword as the ideal defensive and offensive weapon of its era. Roman soldiers who used the two-edged sword called it the "Drinker of Blood."

The Power of His Word

Do you realize God upholds and maintains all things through the power of His Word?[243] Since we are created in His image and have His Spirit living in us, shouldn't we do the same?

---

239. Psalm 1:3
240. Psalm 12:6
241. John 6:63
242. John 1:1
243. Hebrews 1:3

"He was clothed with a robe dipped in blood, and His name is called The Word of God" (Revelation 19:13). When Jesus returns and leads the armies of heaven, He will be known as the Word of God.[244] How awesome is that? And on His thigh will be written King of Kings and Lord of Lords.[245] Hallelujah!

This is the importance God places on His Word.

> And He said, "The kingdom of God is as if a man should scatter seed on the ground, and should sleep by night and rise by day, and the seed should sprout and grow, he himself does not know how. For the earth yields crops by itself: first the blade, then the head, after that the full grain in the head." (Mark 4:26–28)

Jesus said that His Word is like a seed.[246] We plant His Word by speaking it forth from our mouths and believing what we are saying in our hearts. Once we do this, we usually have to wait a while for the seeds to sprout and grow. It is important for us not to grow weary waiting for it because we will reap a harvest of blessings if we do not give up.[247]

After we have spoken our words of faith, we can expect the devil to counterattack us.[248] He will drop his negative thoughts into our minds. "You can't do that! You don't have the education or the training for it! You have always failed in the past and you will continue to fail in the future!"

This is when we must open our mouths and fight. "Oh, yes I can. I have a Christ-like mind.[249] The Holy Spirit is my teacher and He teaches me all things.[250] I can do all things through Christ who strengthens me.[251] And God always leads me in triumph."[252]

---

244. Revelation 19:13
245. Revelation 19:16
246. Luke 8:11
247. Galatians 6:9
248. Mark 4:17
249. 1 Corinthians 2:16
250. John 14:26
251. Philippians 4:13
252. 2 Corinthians 2:14

THE WEAPONS OF A WARRIOR

Yes, we have had years of speaking and agreeing with the world and being deceived by the devil, but with the help of the Holy Spirit, we can change. Speaking His Word over our circumstances will accelerate our harvests.

For example, we can speed up our healing by speaking God's healing words over our bodies and coming into agreement with His Word. I have written and said it often how I used to take a hundred and fifty pills per month, but now I take none. I was the poster child for depression, but now He has set me free and His joy fills my heart. I love boasting on the Lord and what He can do when we follow His ways. What His Word has done for me, it will do for you, too.

We can bring increase into our finances by decreeing and declaring what the Word of God has to say about prosperity. I'm a witness to that, too. Speaking His Word works! Thank you, Jesus!

When we pray and ask God for something, we are confessing God's Word, but in order for it to sprout and grow into a harvest, we must water it. We do this by praising Him and backing it up with His Word. It only takes a few minutes to look up scriptures which agree with our needs and then to speak them forth. It's not necessary to pray and ask Him again about our needs because He heard us the first time we prayed. His ears are always open to our cries.[253]

"Ask boldly, believingly, without a second thought. People who 'worry their prayers' are like wind-whipped waves. Don't think you're going to get anything from the Master that way, adrift at sea, keeping all your options open" (James 1:6–8 MSG). Worrying, pleading and whining won't get God's attention. It is our faith in His Word that gets His attention and moves Him on our behalf. It's kind of like what the farmer does after he plants his seed in the field. He has to continue tending the crop by weeding and watering it, but the farmer doesn't plant it again, does he? He waits until it reaches maturity. Then he harvests his crop.

Some of my prayers were answered almost right away, some took days, some weeks, some months, and a few took years. Like the farmer,

253. Psalm 34:17

138

we have to wait patiently for our seeds of faith to reach maturity so we can harvest them.

But we have to be careful not to dig up our seeds of faith up with negative words of doubt.

For example, let's say we've been praying and asking for a pay raise at our workplace. We can water our prayer by saying, "Lord, I thank You that according to Your Word in Psalms 75:6, promotion does not come from the East nor the West, but from You; You lift up one and put down another. So I thank You that You are lifting me up. I thank You that You are showing me favor on my job. For You said that Your favor surrounds me as a shield."[254]

This is how you decree and declare, calling those things that do not exist as though they did.[255]

Let me show you how our words can dig up our seeds of faith.

Let's say you prayed for a promotion at work, but nothing seems to be happening. Maybe business has even turned for the worse and the company has begun laying people off. What does the devil do? He points out what's happening, causing panic in your heart.

Perhaps you end up saying, "Well, I guess there is no need for me to keep believing for a promotion. I'll be lucky if I can keep my job, let alone being promoted. As a matter of fact, maybe I'd better start looking for something else, just in case I lose my job."

Remember, we plant our seeds with our faith-filled words, but we also dig them up with our negative words. We must hold fast to our confession of faith, trusting God is able to do what we have asked Him to do.[256]

"Your own mouth condemns you, and not I; yes, your own lips testify against you" (Job 15:6). Our negative words will destroy our prayers. You see, it is impossible to please God without faith.[257] "You will also declare a

---

254. Psalm 5:12
255. Romans 4:17
256. Hebrews 4:14
257. Hebrews 11:6

thing, and it will be established for you; so light will shine on your ways" (Job 22:28). Speaking words of faith will always profit us.[258] Hallelujah!

Our Flesh Profits Nothing

"It is the Spirit Who gives life [He is the Life-giver]; the flesh conveys no benefit whatever [there is no profit in it]. The words (truths) that I have been speaking to you are spirit and life" (John 6:63 AMP). We must become Word-dependent, but sadly, many believers are still flesh-dependent, even though Jesus said there is no profit in our flesh. His Word is Spirit and life, backed by His power.

We can pray for our sicknesses, we can speak to our sicknesses and command them to go, but if we are still in pain, our flesh will scream at us. What will we do next? It's our choice. We have the power of life and death in our tongues.[259]

"He who would love life and see good days, let him refrain his tongue from evil, and his lips from speaking deceit" (1 Peter 3:10). We must watch the words we speak. It is entirely up to us to guard our tongues.

I always write down the things God speaks to me and then I confess them every day until they come to pass. One of the things He first spoke to me was about my radio ministry. I wrote His words down and added the date, September 29, 2006, next to them. He gave me scriptures to back up His words. I then wrote out a declaration, which I began speaking almost every day.

"Lord, I thank You that that I am like a tree that has been firmly rooted and planted by streams and rivers of living water. Therefore I will bring forth fruit in my season.[260] Lord, I thank You that my season is here and my appointed time is now. God, thank you for opening up doors for me.[261] Thank You that You have given me favor in heaven and with all mankind.[262] For You said that as Jesus had favor with You and

---

258. Hebrews 4:2
259. Proverbs 18:21
260. Psalm 1:3
261. 1 Corinthians 16:9
262. Isaiah 22:22; Proverbs 3:4

140

all mankind and as He was on this earth so am I on this earth now.[263] Father, I thank You that just as Esther was called for such a time, so I believe that I also have been called for such a time as this.[264] I have faith that I am doing what You have ordained me to do. I pray that you will continue to direct my steps and keep me on the path that You have laid out for me.[265] Thank you, Lord, for the doors that you have opened for me, for the opportunity to teach the Word of Life to thousands and to the nations. I thank you for giving me the desires of my heart, the largest desire being to teach thousands at one time, to minister hope to the lost, and set the captives free.[266] Father, I thank you that my vats overflow, my harvest is here; so be it in Jesus' name, Amen."

That was my prayer and confession. I started confessing it in 2006 and continued doing it in 2007, 2008, 2009, 2010, and 2011. In April of 2011, I finally went on a radio station. It took a while, but His Word came to pass in my life.

My friend, what the Lord has done for me, He will do for you, too.

Prayer

Father, reveal to my friend the power of Your Word and that it is truly a two-edged sword, able to pierce to the division of our souls and spirits. Also, give my friend the boldness to speak Your Word to every mountain in his life. In Jesus' name, Amen.

263. 1 John 4:17
264. Esther 4:14
265. Psalm 37:23; Psalm 20:24
266. Psalm 37:4

Chapter 12
Winning the War of Words

S ome of the most critical moments in our lives occur right after we have been blindsided by a spiritual attack. The first words we speak may determine the outcome of our battles. Of course, the words we speak depend totally on what we having been feeding our spirits. If we have been feeding on fear and doubt, that is what we will speak with our words. But if we have been feeding our spirits with His Word, we will speak God's Word at our circumstances.

"A good person produces good things from the treasury of a good heart, and an evil person produces evil things from the treasury of an evil heart. What you say flows from what is in your heart" (Luke 6:45 NLT). No matter what the devil throws at us, God has scriptures for us to speak which will release His power to help us become overcomers in our conflicts.[267] It's up to us to continually refuel our spirits with His Word.

Thus, in order to win fights of faith, we must first win the war of words. We must learn not limit the Holy One of Israel if we want to walk in victory.[268]

Do you remember David's battle with Goliath? Do you realize his battle did not begin with the Philistine giant but with King Saul?

On that particular day, young David was acting like most of us in our everyday lives. He was running errands for his father Jesse by bringing

267. Romans 8:37
268. Psalm 78:41

roasted grain, loaves of bread, and cheese to his three brothers, who had joined Israel's army.[269] The Israeli army was gathered together to fight the Philistines.[270]

Fighting a giant Philistine had to be the furthest thought from David's mind. He was there to drop off supplies, check on his brothers, and hurry home to give a report to his father.

But while he visited his three brothers, Goliath appeared on the hill opposite Israel's army and challenged Israel by saying, "I defy the armies of Israel today! Send me a man who will fight me!"[271]

Goliath's words frightened the Israeli soldiers into fleeing the battlefield.[272] David overheard a soldier's words about King Saul's offer of a reward for killing the Philistine.[273] The youth began asking other soldiers about the reward. His questions were reported to King Saul, who sent for him.

> "Don't worry about this Philistine," David told Saul. "I'll go fight him!"

> "Don't be ridiculous!" Saul replied. "There's no way you can fight this Philistine and possibly win! You're only a boy, and he's been a man of war since his youth."

> But David persisted. "I have been taking care of my father's sheep and goats," he said. "When a lion or a bear comes to steal a lamb from the flock, I go after it with a club and rescue the lamb from its mouth. If the animal turns on me, I catch it by the jaw and club it to death. I have done this to both lions and bears, and I'll do it to this pagan Philistine, too, for he has defied the armies of the living God! The Lord who rescued me from the

269. 1 Samuel 17:17–18
270. 1 Samuel 17:1–2
271. 1 Samuel 17:10 NLT
272. 1 Samuel 17:24
273. 1 Samuel 17:25

claws of the lion and the bear will rescue me from this Philistine!" (1 Samuel 17:32–37)

Some people lose their battles before the war even begins, but not young David. He spoke faith-filled words and refused to be intimidated by Goliath's size. David saw the giant as a mortal man, who had defied the living God.[274] He looked at the situation from God's point of view and not through his own eyes. David even refused to pay attention to King Saul's doubts and answered the king with his faith-filled logic.

> For though we walk in the flesh, we do not war according to the flesh. For the weapons of our warfare are not carnal but mighty in God for pulling down strongholds, casting down arguments and every high thing that exalts itself against the knowledge of God, bringing every thought into captivity to the obedience of Christ. (2 Corinthians 10:3–5)

A stronghold is an area of darkness within our minds that causes ongoing spiritual, emotional, or behavioral problems for us. These strongholds can defeat us when we wage war against the devil. This can happen to any of us, even if we are born again and sincere in our faith. We can pull our strongholds down with His Word. Hallelujah!

If David had any strongholds in his mind about his battle with Goliath on that day, his faith-filled words swept all of them away. The youth must have known his mouth was an important weapon for him.[275] "Saul finally consented. 'All right, go ahead,' he said. 'And may the Lord be with you!'" (1 Samuel 17:37 NLT).

After David tried on and then rejected King Saul's armor, David chose five smooth stones, put them in his shepherd's bag, picked up his staff and sling, and headed out to face Goliath.[276]

> Goliath walked out toward David with his shield bearer ahead of him, sneering in contempt at this ruddy-faced

274. 1 Samuel 17:36
275. Psalm 12:6
276. 1 Samuel 17:40

boy. "Am I a dog," he roared at David, "that you come at me with a stick?" And he cursed David by the names of his gods. "Come over here, and I'll give your flesh to the birds and wild animals!" Goliath yelled.

David replied to the Philistine, "You come to me with sword, spear, and javelin, but I come to you in the name of the Lord of Heaven's Armies—the God of the armies of Israel, whom you have defied. Today the Lord will conquer you, and I will kill you and cut off your head. And then I will give the dead bodies of your men to the birds and wild animals, and the whole world will know that there is a God in Israel! And everyone assembled here will know that the Lord rescues his people, but not with sword and spear. This is the Lord's battle, and he will give you to us!" (1 Samuel 17:41–47 NLT)

David did not say that *he* was going to conquer Goliath; instead he said, "Today, the Lord will conquer you." His faith was in God, not in himself. He understood that it was God who would fight the battle and give him the victory.

"As Goliath moved closer to attack, David quickly ran out to meet him" (1 Samuel 17:48 NLT). David did not hesitate, but ran straight toward Goliath. As David ran, he reached into his shepherd's bag for a stone, placed the stone in his sling, and hurled it at Goliath. The stone hit the giant in the forehead and killed him.

So David triumphed over the Philistine with only a sling and a stone, for he had no sword. Then David ran over and pulled Goliath's sword from its sheath. David used it to kill him and cut off his head. When the Philistines saw that their champion was dead, they turned and ran. (1 Samuel 17:50–51 NLT)

Like David, we have to realize the battle is the Lord's and that we must win the war of the words with our mouths.

Speaking The Word Properly

Many people don't realize that most of their prayers are not very good. Yes, their prayers sound religious to everyone's ears, but they don't pray according to God's Word. I understand this problem quite well because I used to pray the same type of prayers for myself. I would pray, "Lord, I pray You are going to heal my arm. You are going to do this or You're going to do that." And nothing ever happened.

Then, as I studied His Word, I realized every word written in the Bible is in the past tense. It has already been done. So, now when I pray for my healing, I say, "Lord, by Your stripes I am healed. Thank You for healing me. In Jesus' name, Amen."

"Who Himself bore our sins in His own body on the tree, that we, having died to sins, might live for righteousness—by whose stripes you were healed" (1 Peter 2:24). Even after I received this revelation, it was a process; it took time to change my words to agree with His Word, but I finally got it. Praise the Lord!

This became more and more important because the Lord would whisper things to me. I would write them in a book and begin confessing them. I remember the time I wrote what God was going to do for me and He corrected me. He told me that He had already done it for me. "I'm sorry, Lord. Forgive me," I said. Then, I rubbed the words out and wrote that the Lord had already done it. It's a done deal. It's on the way. And it did happen!

It would not have happened if I had not changed my words. Whatever we ask, He answers the moment we pray.[277] That's when we receive it by faith and go from the asking mode to the thanksgiving mode until it shows up.

It is OK to say something like, "Lord, I thank You it's done even though it looks worse than ever, but in the name of Jesus I declare it is done."

I still remember when the Lord dropped the idea into my spirit about becoming the chaplain at Duplin Correctional Center in North Carolina.

277. Mark 11:24

It was about a year before I really acted on it, but the Lord kept dropping it back into my spirit. He did this until I couldn't ignore it anymore.

The devil pounced each time the Lord whispered to my heart about being a chaplain. The devil had a long list of reasons why I wasn't qualified. Why did he do this? He wanted to steal the Word from me and interrupt God's plan for my life.[278]

From a natural standpoint, the devil was correct. North Carolina required specific training, which I did not have. But the truth is that the devil only told me half-truths, because it wasn't what I could do, but what God could do. God did not ask for my résumé—He already knew all about my abilities and training.

The only qualification I had from a human point of view was that I was an ordinary minister. Some of my friends even told me that I probably wasn't going to get it. A few even said, "Well, sister, I just don't know. You never did this and that and you know, they are pretty strict about these things here in North Carolina."

"Well," I replied, "it's a battle just like with Goliath and David. It was Goliath said, David said, Goliath said, and David said. The devil says, you say. The devil says, you say."

The good news is that when we stand by faith, we get to say the last word, right? I told them, "I believe the Lord placed the idea about me being a chaplain in my spirit. If I am correct, and I believe I am, then I will be the chaplain."

A few months later, I became the chaplain and worked there until the Lord brought me to Virginia to start Speak the Word Ministries. No training! I was the first chaplain to ever be hired in North Carolina without any training.

Proper Perspective

"I can do all things through Christ who strengthens me" (Philippians 4:13). If I would have listened to the devil, I would have never become

---

278. Mark 4:15

a chaplain; nor would I be a Bible teacher today. My qualifications were not much back then.

When I became a Christian, I knew one verse, but God set me aside for a couple of years and taught me lots of them. He armed me and said, "Now, you go get them."

"OK, Lord, we are going to go get them," I replied.

Today, I still write down what He speaks to my spirit. I confess it until it comes to pass. It doesn't matter if it is healing, finances, my children, salvation for others, or whatever, I keep speaking it because I know it works.

Not long ago, I felt the Lord wanted me to call my son, for whom I had been praying for years about his salvation. David and I were in the car, riding back from my nephew's wedding. I told David, "I feel in my spirit that I need to call Doug right now." He agreed with me.

I phoned my son. He answered and we talked for a few minutes. "Mom," he eventually said, "you couldn't have called me at a better moment. I'm really having a hard time."

He ended up giving his life to the Lord over the phone that day. Praise the Lord!

Sometimes we lose our battles because we don't have the right perspective about them. David gave Saul his qualifications for fighting Goliath and that he knew the outcome of the battle ahead of time. He would kill the Philistine. His battles with the bear and lion had prepared him for the giant. His confidence and trust were in God. Nothing is impossible for Him.[279]

Maybe we have enough faith to heal a headache right now. But if we keep persisting, who knows? Perhaps we will be able to soon heal people of cancer and diabetes. We have to start with the small things first and then move forward to higher levels of faith.[280]

---

279. Matthew 19:26
280. Zechariah 4:10

THE WEAPONS OF A WARRIOR

David spoke the outcome of the battle before he fought Goliath because he believed God would deliver him from the giant in the same way He had from the bear and lion. This is called mountain-moving faith!

My friend, think about that for a moment. If the Lord has delivered you out of your last trial, He hasn't changed, right? He is the same yesterday, today, and forever.[281] So He will put you back on top of the mountain again and again.

David was one of the great prophets of Israel.[282] Was his prediction about killing Goliath his first prophecy? We don't know for sure. Scripture only tells us he was a shepherd boy who loved to sing and praise God, but it does not mention any prophecies before this day.[283]

There was another important thing David did before his battle. He refused to allow the devil to have the last word. Goliath spoke his negative words, but then David spoke words of faith to counter Goliath's words. David's words were backed by God Almighty who tells us, "I am alert and active, watching over My word to perform it."[284]

"So shall My word be that goes forth from My mouth; it shall not return to Me void, but it shall accomplish what I please, and it shall prosper in the thing for which I sent it" (Isaiah 55:11). When we speak His Word, we are sending it out to do something, whether it is for our healing, finances, jobs, salvation, or our family. The Word will not return void to God without accomplishing what He wants it to do. We must believe this!

If Satan whispers doubts to our hearts, trying to intimidate us, we must keep pushing forward. "Therefore submit to God. Resist the devil and he will flee from you" (James 4:7). We submit ourselves to God by speaking His Word and speaking to our mountains. Sometimes I voice my resistance to the devil by saying, "Satan, I resist you in the name of Jesus."

281. Hebrews 13:8
282. Acts 2:30
283. 1 Samuel 16:11
284. Jeremiah 1:12 AMP

150

I am living proof that this works, but I also want to warn you that the devil will keep coming back again and again. He will continue trying to plant doubts and fears into your heart. He is persistent!

> Then Jesus, full of the Holy Spirit, returned from the Jordan River. He was led by the Spirit in the wilderness, where he was tempted by the devil for forty days. Jesus ate nothing all that time and became very hungry.
>
> Then the devil said to him, "If you are the Son of God, tell this stone to become a loaf of bread."
>
> But Jesus told him, "No! The Scriptures say, 'People do not live by bread alone.'"
>
> Then the devil took him up and revealed to him all the kingdoms of the world in a moment of time. "I will give you the glory of these kingdoms and authority over them," the devil said, "because they are mine to give to anyone I please. I will give it all to you if you will worship me."
>
> Jesus replied, "The Scriptures say, 'You must worship the Lord your God and serve only him.'"
>
> Then the devil took him to Jerusalem, to the highest point of the Temple, and said, "If you are the Son of God, jump off! For the Scriptures say, 'He will order his angels to protect and guard you. And they will hold you up with their hands so you won't even hurt your foot on a stone.'"
>
> Jesus responded, "The Scriptures also say, 'You must not test the Lord your God.'"
>
> When the devil had finished tempting Jesus, he left him until the next opportunity came. (Luke 4:1–13 NLT)

Kenneth Hagin said, "If you have a Bible that you can't write in, get rid of it! Get yourself one you can write in."

I took Hagin's advice. I underlined in my Bible every place the devil said something in this set of verses and every place where Jesus responded to him. I did this to remind myself of the importance of speaking His Word. Did you notice it took three responses from Jesus to get rid of the devil? We can expect the devil to be just as determined with us. So keep speaking His Word.

Reinhard Bonnke said the Lord told him, "My Word in your mouth is just as powerful as My Word is in My mouth." Now, that is something to shout about. Hallelujah!

Prayer

Father, reveal to my friend that she is always more than a conqueror when she trusts in You and when she speaks Your Words at her mountains. Give her the boldness of the Lion of Judah in her battles with the devil.

Chapter 13
Taking the Limits Off God

How many more days are we willing to put up with problems in our lives? How much longer are we willing to be sick? How much longer are we willing to not have enough finances to cover our needs? How much longer before we begin speaking to our mountains and using the authority God has given us to be set free?

It's up to us to do something, not Him. He has furnished us with every spiritual blessing we will ever need.[285]

But perhaps we are like Pharaoh.

Most of us are familiar with the ten plagues God brought upon Egypt. The first plague was turning the water in the Nile to blood.[286] The second plague was the one with the frogs.[287]

Moses went to Pharaoh and said, "If you don't let God's people go, the Nile River will swarm with frogs. They will come up out of the river and into your palace. They will be in your bed, your oven, your food, on you, and everywhere."[288]

Pharaoh ignored Moses' warning because his magicians could also cause frogs to come out of the Nile.[289] More frogs!

---

285. Ephesians 1:3
286. Exodus 7:17
287. Exodus 8:2
288. Exodus 8:3
289. Exodus 8:7

Then Pharaoh summoned Moses and Aaron and begged, "Plead with the Lord to take the frogs away from me and my people. I will let your people go, so they can offer sacrifices to the Lord."

"You set the time!" Moses replied. "Tell me when you want me to pray for you, your officials, and your people. Then you and your houses will be rid of the frogs. They will remain only in the Nile River."

"Do it tomorrow," Pharaoh said.

"All right," Moses replied, "it will be as you have said. Then you will know that there is no one like the Lord our God. (Exodus 8:8–10 NLT)

Pharaoh could have asked to have the plague of frogs stopped right then and there. He didn't have to sleep one more night with frogs in his bed, crawling all over him. It was his decision to wait until the next day.

The same is true for us. Why are we waiting? "How great is the goodness You have stored up for those who fear You. You lavish it on those who come to You for protection, blessing them before the watching world" (Psalm 39:19 NLT).

What is our problem? Why are we limiting Him? "Yes, again and again they tempted God, and limited the Holy One of Israel. They did not remember His power: the day when He redeemed them from the enemy" (Psalm 78:41–42).

Psalm 78 lists over eighty things God had done for Israel. He parted the Red Sea.[290] He led Israel by a cloud during the day and a fire at night.[291] He brought streams of water out of a rock.[292] He

---

290. Psalm 78:13
291. Psalm 78:14
292. Psalm 78:16

rained manna on them.[293] He rained meat on them.[294] He worked His wonders in Egypt.[295] Yet they didn't remember His power.[296]

The Israelites may have forgotten God's power, but they remembered how to murmur and complain. They asked questions based on fears and concerns about their own safety: "Can God prepare a table in the wilderness?...Can He give bread also? Can He provide meat for His people?"[297]

Why did they do this?

The Israelites didn't believe God or trust Him to take care of them.[298] These reasons haven't changed much over the centuries because we still struggle with the same ones today.

"For He remembered that they were but flesh, a breath that passes away and does not come again" (Psalm 78:39). God loved Israel! He delivered them anyway because He knew they were not perfect.[299] He knows the same thing about us, too. We mess up all of the time, but He is looking for people who have a heart for Him.[300] Hallelujah!

> "Your words have been harsh against Me," says the Lord, "Yet you say, what have we spoken against You?" You have said, 'It is useless to serve God; what profit is it that we have kept His ordinance, and that we have walked as mourners before the Lord of hosts?' (Malachi 3:13)

It's hard to believe the Israelites saw the signs of the blood, frogs, lice, flies, hail, locusts, and the parting of the Red Sea, but still doubted that God would be there for them. The Israelites suffered from short-term memory loss, but sometimes we do, too.

293. Psalm 78:25
294. Psalm 78:27
295. Psalm 78:43
296. Psalm 78:42
297. Psalm 78:19, 20
298. Psalm 78:22
299. Psalm 78:72
300. 1 Samuel 13:14

My Shopping Testimony

I am a woman who enjoys shopping and like most women, I have a few favorite stores. One of these has a lot of expensive items in it, but I still go to that particular store. Yet there is one department I won't walk through because every item in it is so pricey. I don't even browse in that department. If I happen to think about going into the department, a little voice says, "Jo these things are too expensive for you. You probably should go look in another department."

Has this ever happened to you? Have you ever started to do something and had this little voice say, "Well, I don't know why you are looking at that. You know you can't afford it!"

It still amazes me how I always agreed with the little voice. I would obey it and walk to the other side of the store like a little puppy on a leash.

Maybe a little voice spoke to you much like this, but in a different area of your life. Perhaps it was about a job promotion. The little voice may have told you that you were not qualified because of your lack of education. Did he try to convince you with his reasons? Did you believe him like I did?

The Lord recently whispered to my heart while I listened to a radio program. He revealed I had limited Him by not walking through that entire store. You see, several years ago, I wouldn't even think about walking into the store. I thought it was too expensive for me. Now, I only avoided shopping in one section of it. Isn't that strange?

I guess I believed God could only take me so far, but then I needed to stop. I limited Him. And isn't that what the Israelites did in Psalms 78?

What's the big deal about not being able to shop in certain areas of a store, right? Well, it wasn't about shopping in the store. It was my mindset.

"Seek the Kingdom of God above all else, and live righteously, and he will give you everything you need. So don't be afraid, little flock.

For it gives your Father great happiness to give you the Kingdom" (Luke 12:31–32 NLT). The word "everything" has no limitations in it whatsoever. Praise the Lord!

God does not want to give us only a cupful; He wants to give us an overflowing abundance of what we need. It makes our Father happy to do this for us.

> Look at the lilies and how they grow. They don't work or make their clothing, yet Solomon in all his glory was not dressed as beautifully as they are. And if God cares so wonderfully for flowers that are here today and thrown into the fire tomorrow, he will certainly care for you. Why do you have so little faith? (Luke 12:27–28 NLT)

My mindset had predetermined where I could shop in that store, but this could have been about my finances or a job or healing or my prayers. We must not limit God at all if we want to walk in all of His blessings.

We have to rid ourselves of our small mindsets, which places limits on God. Our God is more than enough. He is El Shaddai.[301] Our Father owns the cattle on a thousand hills and the hills, too.[302] All of the gold and silver are His.[303] And we are His children.[304] Praise the Lord!

Do I believe in being frugal? Of course I do. Yet we can do that without having a poverty mindset.

I certainly have not arrived yet, but I am farther down the road than I was a few years ago. When we arrive in heaven, we will be amazed that the streets are paved in gold.[305] We will have everything we need,

---

301. Exodus 6:2–3
302. Psalm 50:10
303. Haggai 2:8
304. Romans 8:16
305. Revelation 21:21

but we don't have to wait until we get there. We can have more than enough now. Then, we can enjoy our journey to heaven. Hallelujah!

The devil loves to give us the spirit of fear so we won't trust God or His Word. Fear hinders us from moving forward in Him. It is a crippler that will paralyze us and stop us in our tracks.

"My people are destroyed for lack of knowledge" (Hosea 4:6). God wants us to have all the knowledge we need so He can open up the windows of heaven and pour out blessings on us so great that we won't have enough room to contain them all.[306] This is the Father's heart for all of us.

In fact, I often pray, "I thank you, God, that You open up the windows of heaven every day and pour out blessings on me so much that I don't even have room enough to contain them all."

We do not have to feel guilty about praying like this because if He blesses us with abundance, we will have more to give to the kingdom of God.[307] Isn't this what we all want? "The thief comes only in order to steal and kill and destroy. I came that they may have and enjoy life, and have it in abundance [to the full, till it overflows]" (John 10:10 AMP). As children of God we should always be expecting to receive the very best from God.[308] He wants to give us abundance out of His storehouses in heaven.

With the right mindset and a spirit of determination, there are no devils in hell or people on earth who can keep us from the blessings of God or keep us from fulfilling His divine purpose for our lives. We can do all things through Christ who strengthens us, but we must be consistent and faithful.[309] Our hearts must agree with His Word and we must act on it.

---

306. Malachi 3:10
307. 1 Timothy 6:17–18
308. James 1:17
309. Philippians 4:13

Anointed Prayer

Jerry Savelle, an anointed Bible teacher, spoke this prophetic word in 2012: "A year from My goodness you will surely see, and breakthrough after breakthrough, that's how it shall be. So position yourself now so it will happen for you by taking hold of His Word and declaring it's true. Refuse to let go. Don't ever give in, for the best year of your life is about to begin. More favor, more goodness and more blessings too."

I loved this word, but felt it needed to be extended a bit more. So I added: "That's also what 2013 has in store for you and also 2014, 2015, and so on and on and on is what the years have in store for you, too."

Let's keep decreeing and declaring His Word over our lives and circumstances. We don't have to be moved by what we see, but by what we believe.[310] Praise the Lord!

Brother Savelle spoke a different prophetic word in 2004: "My people don't know me as the God of the breakthrough.[311] If they did, they wouldn't be so quick to give up. Tell them the God of breakthrough wants to visit their houses."

This prophetic word is still good for us today. All we need to do is receive it and believe it is true for our own lives.

I make a list of the things that I have asked God for and also I make a list of the things that He tells me. I write them down in a little book and then pray and stand for them until they happen. I mark off each one as I receive them. If they aren't finished in one year, I carry them over to the next year. Seeds don't all mature at the same time. Some come up quickly and others take a little longer.

"For the vision is yet for an appointed time; but at the end it will speak, and it will not lie. Though it tarries, wait for it; because it will surely come, it will not tarry" (Habakkuk 2:3). Each of us needs a

310. 2 Corinthians 5:7
311. 2 Samuel 5:20

vision for our lives. It doesn't matter if our vision is five years old or fifty years old. It will come to pass on its appointed day if we continue to hold onto it by faith. Don't let go!

> Do not, therefore, fling away your [fearless] confidence, for it has a glorious and great reward. For you have need of patient endurance [to bear up under difficult circumstances without compromising], so that when you have carried out the will of God, you may receive and enjoy to the full what is promised. (Hebrews 10:35–36 AMP)

We have to hold on to our promises by faith and not grow weary in doing well.[312] If we do this, we will reap a harvest in due time. Hallelujah!

My friend, here's my question for you: do you want to be in the same place next year? Or do you want something better? The choice is up to you. If you choose to move ahead in God, then you need to change your mindset and remove all of the limitations you have placed on Him. You can do this with God's grace and trusting in His Word.

Sometimes, when I am believing the Lord for certain things, my mind will tell me, "Jo, that's impossible." But I ignore my mind and keep on speaking it anyway.

Not long ago, the Lord whispered to my heart, "Jo, I'm expanding you."

That night, He gave me a bigger room. My first thought when I saw it was, "Well, Lord, I don't know if we can fill this up." Thank God, I kept my mouth shut!

Hey, I am just like everyone else. Doubts hit my mind, but I try to take them captive as soon as possible with His Word.[313] That's what we must do or we will end up limiting God's work in our lives.

---

312. Galatians 6:9
313. 2 Corinthians 10:5

I will open my mouth and declare something like this when doubts hit: "I can do all things through Christ who strengthens me.[314] I thank You Lord that You have predestined and preordained me in the way that I should go.[315] You have prepared in advance the work You have for me to do.[316] I thank You for Your peace right now and that it covers my mind and heart. I can do this because I am more than a conqueror."[317]

This is how we must do it. We must speak aloud at whatever is hitting us at the time. We must stop letting the devil speak his lies to us. He will rob us of our health, our finances, our peace, whatever. It is up to us to wield the sword of the Spirit against him.

Our Image

If we are comparing ourselves to somebody else, we must stop doing that. When I catch myself doing this sort of thing, I say, "Jo, you need to stop this. You'd better talk to yourself."

"For we dare not class ourselves or compare ourselves with those who commend themselves. But they, measuring themselves by themselves, and comparing themselves among themselves, are not wise" (2 Corinthians 10:12). It's not wise for us to compare ourselves with others. When we do this, we put limits on what God can do through us.

Do you remember what happened to the twelve spies Moses sent into the Promised Land?[318] Ten came back with bad reports and two had good reports. Why did the ten men have bad reports?

> "We can't go up against them! They are stronger than we are!" So they spread this bad report about the land among the Israelites: "The land we traveled through and explored will devour anyone who goes to live there.

---

314. Philippians 4:13
315. Romans 8:29–30
316. Ephesians 2:10
317. Romans 8:37
318. Exodus 13:2

All the people we saw were huge. We even saw giants there, the descendants of Anak. Next to them we felt like grasshoppers, and that's what they thought, too!" (Numbers 13:31–33 NLT)

The ten spies compared themselves to the inhabitants of the land. They forgot who was on their side—the Lord God of Hosts. They saw themselves as failures before they had even begun their journey. It didn't matter that Caleb and Joshua spoke words of faith because the ten spies' words of fear crippled the whole nation of Israel.[319]

"Fear gripped me, and my bones trembled" (Job 4:14). Let's not allow fear to limit what God can do through us. We are more than conquerors through Christ and He will always lead us in triumph.[320] All we need to do is trust Him and speak His Word at our mountains.

Prayer

Father, may grace and peace be multiplied to my friend in the knowledge of You and of Jesus our Lord.[321] May he be a doer of the Word and put into action everything he has learned in this book so that he will prosper in all things and be in good health, even as his soul prospers.[322]

Two Prayers and Declarations

People contact me all the time requesting that I give them a prayer or declaration over specific areas that they're struggling in. I intend to eventually write an entire book of prayers and declarations. For now, I

319. Numbers 14:7–10
320. 2 Corinthians 2:14
321. 2 Peter 1:2
322. 3 John 2

would like to leave you with two that I consider to be the most important in our walk with God:

Stopping Satan

> Now whom you forgive anything, I also forgive. For if indeed I have forgiven anything, I have forgiven that one for your sakes in the presence of Christ, lest Satan should take advantage of us; for we are not ignorant of his devices. (2 Corinthians 2:10–11)

My Prayer

Lord, I thank You for opening my eyes and illuminating my understanding to recognize Satan's attacks against my life. I am so grateful that You have sent the Holy Spirit to be my Teacher and Guide and to equip me to stand against every assault that comes against my life, my family, and all of my relationships. Thank You for arming me with the power and insight of the Spirit, and because of this I never have to allow the enemy to take advantage of me again. In Jesus' name, Amen.

My Confession

I declare that I am no longer ignorant of Satan's devices because the Holy Spirit is my Teacher and Helper. Therefore the enemy never has an advantage over me in his battles against me because the Spirit of Truth shows me things to come, even the strategies of the devil. I declare that I will continue to fight the good fight, finish the race, and keep the faith until the day I meet Jesus face to face. I declare this by faith in Jesus' name.

Speaking to Dry Bones

For I will give you a mouth and wisdom which all your adversaries will not be able to contradict or resist. (Luke 21:15)

My Prayer

Father, I thank You for giving me a mouth filled with Your words and wisdom so that my foes and Satan himself will be unable to contradict what I say. Thank You, Father, that You have given me dominion on this earth and over everything in it. I also thank You that Jesus came so I might have an abundant life and that I am seated with Him in a position of authority, far above the darkness and principalities of this world. In Jesus' name, Amen.

My Confession

I declare that no words of doubt and unbelief shall come out of my mouth today. For I shall only speak words of faith and edification. Therefore my words will bring life to every area of my life. I shall speak God's Words of power over every situation that confronts me. I declare that I now take authority over Satan and I break the power of all evil reports spoken against me and my family. I declare that no weapon formed against me shall prosper. I declare all of this in Jesus' Name.

Booklets by
Pastor JoAnne Ramsay

Meet the Author

Pastor JoAnne Ramsay founded Speak the Word Ministries after receiving a visit from the Lord. He instructed her to teach His children how to fight their battles by using His Word and to make it plain and simple so even the most inexperienced Christ-follower could understand. The Lord informed her that His children were engaged in a battle which they were losing because they didn't know how to wield the Sword of the Spirit. Pastor JoAnne's teachings are found in her books, CDs, DVDs, pamphlets, radio shows, and YouTube. Visit her at pastorjoramsay.com.

Order Info

For autographed books, bulk order discounts,
or to schedule speaking engagements, contact:

Pastor JoAnne Ramsay
pastorjoramsay.com
855.505.2297 (toll free)

Also available from your favorite bookstore and Amazon.

Fruitbearer Publishing, LLC
302.856.6649 • FAX 302.856.7742
info@fruitbearer.com
www.fruitbearer.com
P.O. Box 777, Georgetown, DE 19947